D0403489

THE

COMFORT

BOOK

Jane Seskin

Tallfellow®Press

2002

Published by
Tallfellow® Press, Inc.
1180 S. Beverly Drive
Los Angeles, CA 90035

www.tallfellow.com

Designed by SunDried Penguin Design

ISBN 1-931290-18-0

Printed in the United States of America
by Berryville Graphics

10 9 8 7 6 5 4 3 2 1

To all the people who took the time to share memories
and moments of comfort

Acknowledgments

For more than fifteen years I've worked in a special hospital unit that treats victims of violence. There is comfort in the known structure and rhythm of the work. And when it is difficult and draining, my colleagues have been there with encouragement. I thank Sally Clayton, Nilda Lopez, Karen Reichert, Dwarym Ruiz, Anne Skomorowsky and Danette Wilson-Gonzalez for contributing to the richness of my work life on a regular basis.

To my senior team of Andrea Dixon, Ruth Forero, Louise Kindley and Susan Xenarios, I thank you for supporting me when I walk the high wire. We've worked long and well with each other. We've laughed hard, cared deeply and created rich personal and professional memories.

I am grateful to and for the wonderful friends of my heart who've joined me on my different adventures and have offered comfort by their very presence in my life. Thank you, Mary Anderson, Bonnie Burgess, Nancy Garrity, Melissa Mertz, Barbara Niles, Christine Nolin,

Pat Outland, Jane Sinnenberg, Naomi Taicher, Mary Triest and Nicki Turano.

Erika Bernardini Guzman has cheerfully provided technical assistance since the beginning of this project, and what enormous comfort her help has been.

And to my small though stay-in-touch family, I thank Estelle and Erich Arje, David Shapiro and Linda and Kate Breslau.

To all the women I've sat with in Group over 480 Wednesday nights, I thank you for struggling with the concept of comfort, and for trying to find ways to bring it home to yourselves.

Finally, I thank my classmates at the University of Iowa Summer Writing Festivals for their good humor and camaraderie.

Table of Comforts

Introduction

A week after my mother died from a sudden heart attack, a friend asked, "What can I do to comfort you?" It was a simple, caring, generous question to which I had no response. I literally could not think or imagine anything that could soften my grief.

Many years have passed, and I have made a concerted effort to figure out what brings me comfort in general and what comforts me at specific times. I explore what I can do for myself and what I can ask from others. I've also repeated that original question to both friends and clients experiencing sadness, difficulty and emotional distress.

As a psychotherapist working part-time with survivors of domestic violence, the concept of comfort—which I raise during individual and group sessions—is oftentimes a mystery. I'll ask: "What can you do to nourish yourself? What brings you pleasure? What makes you feel better about you, your life, the world?" I've been met with blank stares, averted eyes and a cascade of tears. I've been told, "I don't know. What do you mean? I don't understand the question."

In an effort to learn what comforts people, I sent the short questionnaire at the back of this book to more than five hundred people across the country. I asked friends and colleagues to forward copies of the form to the people in their lives.

Responses came from as far away as England and Germany, from a class of seventh graders in New York, a third-grade chorus in California and the Student Union at the University of Wisconsin.

Personal information was optional. I asked people to describe their occupations or how they'd define themselves. And so for some respondents we have a wonderful, fanciful compilation of realities and dreams. Some chose to answer the questionnaire but leave out their names (anonymous) or identifying information (age, city, occupation).

And for some, resistance to the subject was great. Many, many people had difficulty answering or even talking about comfort. I was told, "It's self-indulgent." "It's too intimate." "I don't have the time for this."

My hunch is that for some people, hard work and survival are the goals, not comfort. Remember the thumb and the "blankie"? They were early, natural, easy comfort items. Then we all grew up, and many of us became so busy helping, caring, giving to others that we forgot how to soothe, take care, nurture, nourish…comfort… our own selves.

And then came 9/11.

I'd just finished an early morning therapy session and picked up my phone messages to hear two friends with almost identical panic in their voices. Each cried out "Turn on the TV!" "Turn on the TV!" And that's how I discovered September 11, a transformative event in this country's history.

It then became important for me to reach out for something to bring me comfort: to continue routines, to contact good friends for limitless conversation and to get plenty of rest while continuing both my therapy practice and new work with survivors and family members of 9/11.

Looking back, I remember getting great satisfaction from reading stacks of home furnishing magazines. Obviously, trying to keep my interior calm—both literally and metaphorically.

In those first surreal weeks the warm fall weather allowed me numerous opportunities to sit by my beloved Hudson River and find moments of peace.

I also found comfort in visiting different houses of worship around the city.

A candlelight walk with perhaps fifty neighbors ended at our local firehouse, where we serenaded and applauded the firefighters. This community activity felt right, felt cathartic, felt healing.

When 9/11 occurred, I'd been working on *The Comfort Book* for eighteen months. In the aftermath of the tragedy, a number of people specifically related their entries to that day. There was a focus on a relational connection with others. People spoke of actions that were future oriented and life affirming. They'd consciously chosen to do something, or add something, to their lives. People had sought and found ways to comfort themselves, to move on in the midst of uncertainty and despair.

It's important to note that comfort is not just an emergency bandage to bind up the wounds from bereavement and crisis. It is so much more.

Comfort can be a margin of safety: knowing that a neighbor has your spare set of keys. It can be a measure of trust: that if you become ill you can rely on your health care team, and that your favorite restaurant still delivers.

It's also about nostalgia. Things that evoked pleasure in the past can bring comfort to the present. The tomato soup and grilled cheese sandwiches made by Mom on a rainy day become the comfort food of adulthood.

In times of distress we tend to reach for those foods, places, activities, experiences, and so forth that evoke earlier moments when we felt cared for, full, safe, pleasured.

Comfort is daily action taken to make yourself feel better: reading a book, smelling the fragrance of a flower, soaking in a bubble bath, sitting in silence.

I think it's possible to learn what thoughts, things, places and actions hold out hope and help to soften the hard patches in our lives. What a benefit it is to draw on what has brought feelings of security or happiness in the past, to return to an activity that offers some measure of relief or to try new ideas or new ways to feel good.

This "Comfort Conversation" is one to explore with family and friends. That's my hope for this book.

Jane Seskin
New York City
October 2002

Comfort: *verb* to impart strength and hope; to encourage; to relieve; to console; to cheer; to refresh; to fortify; to support.

noun a state of quiet enjoyment; freedom from pain, want, or anxiety.

The table is a meeting place,

a gathering ground,

the source of sustenance and nourishment,

festivity, safety and satisfaction.

—Laurie Colwin
(author)

Foods

I am so basic it's embarrassing. Anybody who knows me well knows that when I'm cranky or out of sorts, feed me (anything that involves meat, potatoes and gravy) and I'll cheer right up.

—Kathleen, 49, Jersey City, NJ
(social worker)

Cooking is comforting when it can be done right. This means in an empty house with lots of things that need chopping, especially garlic and onions, something bluesy turned up loud on the stereo, and a glass of red wine close at hand. The magic solitude and all the senses satisfied.

—Pat, 48, Lenexa, KS
(creative director)

Chocolate and ice cream make me feel good. I feel safe from hunger because I think of these items as comfort and luxury foods.

—Rick, 48, New York, NY
(social worker)

I make applesauce. I use bruised rejects. Steam them whole until very soft. Mash with a mill. A mix of types makes the color, texture and taste very perky. I eat a bowl of it when it's warm. It's so fundamental, connected with the goodness of the earth. We had apple trees in our yard and used the fallen apples for sauce. Reminds me of a warm, fragrant kitchen, a resourceful mother-pure nourishment. So easy to enjoy gliding down to my very own core.

—Sally, 64, Danbury, CT
(teacher/actress)

I love Cheese Doodles and Chinese food. The crunchy sensation of Cheese Doodles and the spicy warm flavor in Chinese food always puts me in a good mood.

—Anonymous

My favorite sandwiches are grilled cheese and peanut butter and jelly served with tomato rice soup. These were the comfort foods of my childhood.

—Nicki, 32, Muttontown, NY
(mother)

Honey buns are my comfort food of choice because they remind me of the ones my mother used to bake. Born in Russia, long since gone, I would watch her take them out of the oven in a specially ridged muffin pan. The aroma was good, the taste even better. They bring back wonderful warm memories.

—Lew, 67, New York, NY
(retired)

I love the consistency of sourdough bread. The hard crust, the chewiness, the taste. I had it first in the sixties in Berkeley, California, and when I eat it now I'm transported back to those passionate political days of my youth.

—Jane, 57, New York, NY
(psychotherapist/writer)

My favorite comfort food has always been macaroni and cheese because my grandmother made it especially for me when I was a child. She was the one who usually took care of me when I was sick or unhappy.

—Sharon, 55, Lawrence, MA
(children's activities director)

Making and eating chicken soup involves all my senses: sounds of cutting and chopping, peeling, smelling, stirring, tasting, crying (onions), disparate blending of chicken bones and vegetables. The smells permeate the house during hours of simmering on the stove, while I taste at different stages. I sit quietly and enjoy a cup of soup after it's been strained. I sip slowly. Wonderful.

—Mary, 58, Oakland, CA
(singer/music educator)

There's a deep satisfaction and I think a comfort in raising some of your own food—even if it's a small amount. To know that I've planted the seed and tended the growing plant for months and that the result of that labor is this wonderful tomato/onion/cucumber/potato…is to place oneself in the circle of life. It nurtures my spirit, provides a sense of competence and enhances both my feeling of connection and my respect for all those generations before us who somehow managed to survive without supermarkets.

—Howard, 62, Stephenstown, NY
(psychoanalyst)

I've loved ice cream cones since my childhood. I share this love with my father. In the summer, at our country house, we'd walk to a little neighborhood store and buy ice cream cones with sprinkles after dinner. It was a special time for the two of us to talk.

—Marilyn, 52, Fort Lee, NJ
(college professor)

When I'm blue I'll eat something I don't eat often or that I remember from childhood. This makes me feel like I'm really doing something extra for me and the little girl inside. Some of these treats are: chocolate ice cream sodas, root beer floats, chips and dip and cornmeal mush.

—Jan, 51, Cottonwood, AZ
(counselor)

Comfort is a pint of Häagen-Dazs rum raisin ice cream. I don't drink and that's my cheat.

—Elizabeth, 40, New York, NY
(student/mother/volunteer)

I believe that my cooking is a serious kind of self-care. When I get hungry I am grouchy and whiny, just like a little kid. But if I can provide for my calorie needs, I can avoid being a total bitch due to hunger. In the past year, I have been very enthusiastic about Hashbrown Casserole, hash browns and cheese and cream of chicken soup and sour cream, all baked to a golden brown perfection. It's smooth, creamy, warm and cheesy and it has enough fat and other calories to keep me going.

—Gillian, 30, Iowa City, IA
(poet, jester)

Tea—brewed the right way, with real tea leaves, in a pot— preferably served in front of a wood fire. It is a symbol of warmth, comfort and reflection.

—Ellen, 56, Washington, DC
(consultant, international affairs)

I like to cook when I'm feeling upset. I like to make a very detailed recipe. The feeling of doing something that others can enjoy changes my outlook.

—Richard, 48, New York, NY
(teacher)

I need cheese—grilled with extra dill pickles…Swiss on wheat bread with mayonnaise and the obligatory pickles, or, failing that, cheddar—lots of it—on saltine crackers. (I am from the land of cheese and beer—Wisconsin.)

—Sheila, 62, Cincinnati, OH
(photographer)

Peanut butter and jelly (black raspberry!) on soft white bread paired with Campbell's cream of tomato soup. This is certainly not gourmet comfort, but I guess the combination brings back memories of childhood in a comfortable suburban 1950s household. It's a lunch I still have when I'm sick.

—Alan, 55, New York, NY
(college administrator)

When I need comfort I go out to eat. It's a distraction. I order a good sandwich, one that I can wrap my two hands around: a meatball hero with mozzarella. I feel satisfied. Then I go home and take a nap.

—Charles, 17, New York, NY
(student)

Nilla Wafers and tea. One of my best friends (we met in college) is the most comforting, soothing person I've ever known, and whenever I was feeling down I'd go sit with her and she'd make tea with milk and offer me Nilla Wafers. The warmth of the tea and the vanilla flavor always calmed me, but I think her presence had the greater effect. She now lives in Boston while I'm here in New York, and though I can still call her anytime, I can't have her in the room with me at a moment's notice and so the tea and wafers—and their positive association—always make me feel a little better.

—Samantha, 26, New York, NY
(film publicist)

I love to bake bread, from scratch!! I find it so primal, and so basic, to be able to put a few ingredients together and have a magical thing occur. Even kneading the dough helps me to alleviate stress and lose myself in the process of creation. When I bake, the house smells so good it makes me feel sheltered, taken care of and nurtured. It feels like I'm re-creating and reinventing a home for myself each time.

—Nora, 44, Forest Hills, NY
(artist)

WINE. Dry and good, red or white. Of course there is the alcohol. But the whole ritual contributes: opening the bottle, pouring, swirling, eyeing the color, inhaling the, well, taste, for want of a better way of describing it. Sipping, putting down the glass. Especially comforting when conversing with others while sharing the bottle, but works solo, too.

—Rick, 57, Los Angeles, CA
(creator of marketing materials)

A lot has changed since 9/11. New things comfort me now. Things that no one can take away. So…my recipe for Caesar salad dressing. Olive oil—About 2/3 of the whole. I don't like extra virgin, it has a taste of its own. Being a virgin had its own mental pain, but would you wish to be Extra? Fresh lemon juice—A little less then the remaining 1/3. If you can find Meyer lemons, all the better. There's something about the taste. Garlic salt—Lots. Dijon mustard—Maybe a tablespoon. Worcestershire sauce—3 or 4 shakes. Red wine vine-gar—A couple of dashes. Garlic—6 to 8 cloves. Ah, garlic, it's hard to get too much. This is the main secret of this dressing. True, by itself it's just garlic, but mixed together with everything else…va va va voom!! Shredded Parmesan cheese—Mix in with the dressing, with enough left over to cover the top of the salad when ready to serve. No egg—They scare me. Let them grow up and go to work for Colonel Sanders. Croutons—Everyone has their own recipe for really great croutons, feel free. My quick and easy way is to cube a Boboli bread and toast it in the bottom half of a broiling pan with a light sprinkle of olive oil over it. 350 degrees for 20 to 30 minutes.

Crispy on the outside, soft and warm on the inside. The whole thing should be mixed well with cold, hand-torn romaine lettuce. Enjoy with people you love or enjoy by yourself, because if you love anyone, it should be yourself. How could you take comfort from this if you don't?

—Chuck, 68, Oakland, CA
(retired)

I like baking because it's something special my mother would do with us during the holidays. It was a tradition for her to prepare lots and lots of sugar, gingerbread and chocolate chip cookie dough, and then for a few nights in a row we'd (Mom, my siblings and I) make delicious things for our family and friends to enjoy. It used to be that I found comfort in baking simply because I found happiness in eating it. Nowadays I find comfort in baking mostly because I like to give something to people and it is something I do well. I feel that I can somehow put my love for people into what I bake.

—Meghan, 22, Oberlin, OH
(student)

I make a large batch of chocolate chip peanut butter cookies before my family goes on a trip. They keep fresh in a plastic container. So even though we're in new, strange surroundings, the cookies are a familiar and soothing treat from home.

—Carol, 41, Pittsburgh, PA
(lawyer)

I love meals I don't have to prepare; something delivered with lots of carbs is a comfort.

—Anonymous

Comfort is Chinese food—egg rolls, fried dumplings, chicken and broccoli with garlic sauce—on any rainy and cold day, lying on the couch with my lion blanket and watching an old classic on TV like *I'll Cry Tomorrow* or *To Kill a Mockingbird* or *It's a Wonderful Life*.

—Sally, 44, New York, NY
(trance-dance facilitator)

Eggs Benedict and virtually all breakfast foods are comforting. For those with a sweet tooth, try Cheerios with dark brown sugar and heavy cream. Whoa!

—Cathy, 39, Salisbury, CT
(photographer)

I enjoy cooking a creative meal (something spicy and complex), or re-creating an old favorite in a healthier version.

—Danette, 46, Kew Gardens, NY
(restaurant owner/social worker)

Ice cream. Oh, man...it doesn't get much better than ice cream. The stuff is great...what more can I say. You just go out there and do it...you pick up that pint of your favorite flavor...mint chocolate chip or anything in the chocolate family (that doesn't have peanut butter) and you take it home and eat it...in one sitting...from the container. Please...is that perfect or what?

—Darby, 45, Bronx, NY
(drama therapist)

My Comfort Foods

_____

_____

_____

_____

_____

_____

_____

_____

_____

_____

A book is like a garden

carried in the pocket.

—Chinese proverb

Books

I enjoy reading all sorts of biographies. The complexity of people's lives provides comfort. For instance, I really liked *The Chief*, a biography of William Randolph Hearst. I liked how he gambled it all on his newspaper business, even though he started with money. It's an interesting tale of the risks he took.

—Andrew, 32, New York, NY
(broadcast journalist)

I like to re-read mystery novels. The story takes me to another place, and since I already know the ending I'm not so anxious. Talk about escape! Books provide me with knowledge about how my life has been and/or is similar to others. And that is a comfort.

—Valerie, 55, Albany, NY
(museum educator)

When I read I'm transplanted to another place and time, involved in someone else's problems, life, happiness and escape. Some favorites include: *The Notebook* and *A Walk to Remember*, both by Nicholas Sparks, and *Memoirs of a Geisha* by Arthur Golden.

—Nicki, 32, Muttontown, NY
(mother)

I love *Anne of Green Gables* and *The Wind in the Willows*. These books comforted me as a child and continue to live in my memory.

—Anonymous

My father turned me on to mysteries as a kid. He's been gone so long now but reading these books makes me feel a small bit of him is still with me.

—Mary, 53, New York, NY
(health care administrator)

I love cartoon books like *Doonesbury* and *Calvin and Hobbes*.

—Anonymous

I found Rabbi Harold Kushner's book *When Bad Things Happen to Good People* tremendously comforting because he makes such a strong statement that troubles aren't a punishment for being less than perfect. I also love re-reading Tolkien's *Lord of the Rings* trilogy, partly because the littlest people win and partly because it reminds me that even people who seem horrible can somehow cause things to turn out better in the end.

—**Sharon, 55, Lawrence, MA**
(children's activities director)

Jane Eyre by Charlotte Brontë was and still is my favorite book. It's the story of a girl who perseveres in spite of any and all hardships and finds true happiness.

—**Anonymous**

I read meditation books, particularly *God Makes the Rivers to Flow* by Eknath Easwaran. This book contains a wide variety of sayings from philosophers, religious leaders and spiritualists.

—**Richard, 48, New York, NY**
(teacher)

My favorite books for comfort are *The Road Less Traveled*, by M. Scott Peck, M.D. Terrific humanistic insights into life, love and relationships that lead to personal fulfillment and, *The Buddha in Your Mirror: Practical Buddhism and the Search for Self*, by Hochswender, Martin and Morino.

—Eric, 56, West Los Angeles, CA
(financial planner, father/husband/seeker—
not necessarily in that order)

Siddhartha by Herman Hesse is one of my favorite books. His search for his place in life encourages me to look for mine. In addition, I try to read the Bible each day. I believe in God and His ability to hold me and comfort me. I pray to Him and ask Him to fill me with His love.

—Ute, 38, Berlin, Germany
(psychologist)

A favorite book of mine is *Rule of the Bone* by Russell Banks. It's like *The Catcher in the Rye* but with an uplifting, more empowering outcome, one of survival and new meaning.

—Karin, 19, New York, NY
(student/waitress/actress)

What I find comforting above all is great writing, whatever the subject: observations of life from a unique point
of view, huge undertakings, creative mastery of language,
remarkable research which results in mind-boggling
specifics, passion for life and the beauty of it all. So
among my favorite books there's *Crime and Punishment* by
Dostoyevsky; *Winds of War* by Herman Wouk; *All the
Pretty Horses* by Cormac McCarthy; and *Cold Mountain* by
Charles Frazier.

—Tony, 60, New York, NY

The book *Giving the Love That Heals*, by Harville Hendrix
and Helen Hunt, has given me insight into my actions
and choices, inevitably aiding and leading to acceptance
of certain situations and circumstances.

—Anonymous, Cincinnati, OH

I love to read *Winnie-the-Pooh* or any of the *Harry Potter*
books in my snowman pajamas, under my duvet, maybe
with a cup of hot cocoa.

—Jennifer, 40, New York, NY
(professional musician/law student)

I feel the inspirational book, *Man's Search for Meaning,* by Viktor Frankl to be very comforting. It reminds me of the resiliency and raw beauty of our spirit.

—Susan, 55, New York, NY
(program director)

I love to cook and have opened a cooking school in my kitchen, part for profit and part for love. If the house were burning down I would grab…James Peterson's *Fish Cooking.* It's like an encyclopedia. You name the fish and there are several recipes to match it with. And then I'd take Julia Child's *Baking with Julia.* Her recipes are simple, straightforward and delicious. I love it when the house is filled with the smell of baked goods in the morning. And the last choice would be *The Commander's Palace, New Orleans Cookbook* from the restaurant in New Orleans. One, great recipes, great sauces. Two, being originally from Louisiana, it puts me back into my grandmother's kitchen, where something delicious was always cooking.

—Steve, 41, Cold Spring, NY
(property manager)

Writing Down the Bones by Natalie Goldberg was so wonderful and rich to read that I didn't want it to end. On the surface it's about a writer teaching technique and writing exercises, but underneath it's so much more about fully living your life.

—Lauren, 48, Denver, CO
(accountant)

I enjoy the mysteries written by Diane Mott Davidson: *Dying for Chocolate, Killer Pancake, The Cereal Murders.* A caterer is the very human amateur investigator who makes this series special by sharing recipes while solving crimes.

—Jennifer, 33, Montclair, NJ
(jewelry designer)

A Return to Love by Marianne Williamson offers A to Z solutions to life's trials and tribulations. When I read this book it centers me.

—Paul, 37, New York, NY
(makeup artist)

A book that gives me comfort is *Alcoholics Anonymous*, known to some as *The Big Book*. As a recovering alcoholic and drug addict I had to learn to rebuild a relationship with books, which I lost when I began drinking. When I got sober it was suggested that I read some literature and that led me to *The Big Book*. At first I picked it up as I was going to sleep to calm the frazzled nerves that were still used to getting drink signals. I would open the book to any page and just begin reading. Books became friends the longer I stayed sober. In truth, everything got better in my life, of course, but I found myself drawn to *The Big Book* as it became a great comfort and a safety zone, Within the blue-bound covers were the stories of people just like me; alcoholics who had found a way, one day at a time, to live without a drink.

—Sherry, 55, New York, NY
(administrative assistant)

After a period of stress and overcommitment I like Sir Arthur Conan Doyle's Sherlock Holmes stories, because of their solid sense of order, justice and good values.

—Ellen, 56, Washington, DC
(consultant, international affairs)

I enjoy mystery novels because they allow me to be taken away into a very different time and place. I become consumed, a kind of intimate involvement with the characters and the plot such that my life as a husband, father, analyst, son, brother, etc. and all the responsibilities that come with the above are temporarily suspended. I have to completely focus on what I'm reading. I ultimately find that very relaxing.

—Shelly, 53, New York, NY
(psychologist)

I find reading classic British detective fiction (P. D. James, Sarah Caudwell) to be comforting because it's witty and wry and challenges my deductive powers!

—Victoria, 32, New York, NY
(researcher)

My favorite book is *Le Petit Prince* by Saint-Exupery. For me it's a "parable" on life, wisdom, simplicity and friendship. What's truly important!

—Maria, 60, Cambridge, MA

When I need comfort I find myself reading Scriptures in the Bible. This brings me warmth, love and guidance. At times, I hold the Bible in my hands, close my eyes and open up to any page and start to read what's before me.

—Elena, 25, New York, NY
(angel without wings)

Books have always represented a vicarious family to me. I can be involved with the characters and understand their pain and suffering. I read a lot and it often keeps loneliness at bay. I like every writer that is good with words and builds characters that seem to be in the room with me. I loved a book called *We Band of Angels* by Elizabeth Norman. It's about the nurses that were prisoners of war as a result of serving on Bataan and Corregidor [both in the Phillipines]. I loved *The Red Tent* by Anita Diamant, for its caring fictionalized picture of ancient womanhood. I like anything by Robert Ludlum unless he was trying to be funny. His plots are complex with a lot of suspense. He didn't know me from a hole in the ground, but I felt that I had lost a friend when he died last year.

—Jackie, 63, Bloomington, IL
(nurse/teacher)

For pure mindless reading enjoyment I like the science fiction author Piers Anthony. Although he has some material that takes a great deal of thought, his *Mundania* series is based entirely upon puns. I also enjoyed a book entitled *Riddley Walker* by Russell Hoban. The book is written phonetically, which meant it took me about three pages to learn to read, then completely messed up my spelling for weeks after finishing it. Nothing deep about my reading. I use it as a release so it's generally extremely light.

—Rich, 35, Highland, IN
(graphic designer)

Reading biographies about incredibly brave people is mesmerizing and uplifting. I particularly think of *Ice Bound* by Jerri Nielsen (the doctor who discovered her own breast cancer while she was stationed at the South Pole). It was inspirational.

—Robin, 50, New York, NY
(psychotherapist)

My Comfort Books

_____

_____

_____

_____

_____

_____

_____

_____

_____

_____

Life is a great big canvas;

throw all the paint on it you can.

—*Danny Kaye*
(comedian)

Places

Being in the mountains at night, in front of a campfire, talking about life with old people feels comforting, because I'm sharing and learning from those with experience.

—Patricio, 32, Torres del Paine, Chile
(tour guide)

Visiting churches, cemeteries and other quiet places gives me the sense that I am part of something larger than myself.

—Christine, 49, New York, NY
(social worker)

I love going to the library, a place that feels safe but one that also provides opportunities to enter "other worlds."

—Valerie, 55, Albany, NY
(museum educator)

It comforts me to go to a supermarket and think about what I could buy for dinner that the people I love would enjoy eating. A good food store exists as a resource for potential happiness, and the person who enters it as a customer is removed from any other care except the responsibility of choosing what he knows he can prepare that will nourish people and make them happy. The multitude of choices in a supermarket is a world apart, the backstage area of daily life.

—Jeff, 56, Cold Spring, NY
(writer)

We got sent home early from work after the Pentagon was bombed on September 11. I couldn't wait to get back to my apartment. To get inside. To feel safe. I felt numb. I sat on my couch for hours watching TV, holding and petting my cat. Slowly, over the course of the day, I began to feel a bit calmer. I know the comfort came because I was in my own beloved space with my own dear pet on my lap.

—Beth, 31, Arlington, VA
(secretary)

I was born in Puerto Rico and came to the States as a child. Visiting Puerto Rico is a great comfort. Whenever my wife and I go on vacation there I feel so at peace. It's the clear water, the weather, waterfalls and the *Coquís* (little frogs that say their name).

—Ramon, 35, New York, NY
(network administrator)

When I'm very depressed about a personal trauma, my source of comfort is to create a feeling where I am part of the universe, and so my problems seem small in comparison. How to do this? If there's a beach nearby, the rhythm of the waves is soothing. The repetition of the waves, no matter what happens with people on earth, coupled with the sheer power of the ocean is very comforting.

—Susan, 51, Lawrence, MA
(realtor)

I've been visiting aquariums all my life. Watching fish glide through water is relaxing for me.

—Anonymous

Amusement parks are fun. Roller coasters comfort me by making me feel youthful and childlike.

—Rick, 48, New York, NY
(social worker)

I go back to my birthplace and all the negative feelings I've been carrying around are lifted away. It's like I've been reborn and I feel just great.

—Anonymous

For comfort I head to the beach/shore...doing anything (bicycle riding) or nothing (simply contemplating the ocean and waves). The sounds and smell of the ocean and the simplicity of other people's activities (fishing, swimming, sunning, etc.) help to reorient me and remind me that life's joys, by and large, derive from simple, basic things and not from the complexities that we've created for ourselves.

—Gary, 49, Manhattan Beach, CA
(investment adviser, parent of 3 teenagers)

I like going to church, feeling part of a group of people who keep trying to get it right.

—Rosie, 51, Stamford, CT
(retired)

I go to the beach in the fall and in the winter. There's almost no one there to bother you, and just sitting and watching the water can be very tranquilizing.

—Anonymous

My favorite spot in the world is Jamaica. This is where my youngest and fondest memories are located. Whenever life is difficult for me I try to remember those early days.

—Valicia, Brooklyn, NY
(executive secretary)

Going to a cathedral or Catholic church in between serv-ices is comforting because of the hushed quality, the flicker and warmth of the burning candles, being around others who are praying or meditating.

—Anonymous

I sit in Starbucks at the end of a hectic day, sip coffee, listen to music and catch up on "pleasure reading"…it can be either personal or professional, but only stuff I've been wanting to read for a while.

—Eric, 56, West Los Angeles, CA
(financial planner, father/husband/seeker—
not necessarily in that order)

I've got this Lotus sofa by my kitchen window that looks out on the sky and a willow tree. I go there sometimes with something to read, or maybe just to take a nap. Comfortable.

—Peter, 31, Brooklyn, NY
(teacher)

I go to four to six spiritual retreats a year lasting from a weekend to ten days. When I am there (a monastery, conference center) I am able to enter a meditative state where I am free of all anxiety. I am nourished by the surroundings, the food, the people. I find a place back to myself.

—Michelle, 59, New York, NY
(psychotherapist/minister)

Put me on a train by a window and I'm happy. I've
watched the scenery change going cross-country. I've
seen the fall colors riding through New England, and
going from Quebec to Montreal in first class was sheer
comfort and elegance.

—Jane, 57, New York, NY
(psychotherapist/writer)

When everything hits the wall, I need the inside of a
quiet church, not an antiseptic modern area, but a real
church with candles and the statues of saints who've
made it through bad times themselves. Generally, I throw
my prayers at the Blessed Mother because it's a mother's
comfort, a mother's arms I need around me.

—Sheila, 62, Cincinnati, OH
(photographer)

Going to my country house on a lake in Massachusetts
brings me comfort. I go out alone in my blow-up row-
boat to the middle of the lake and rest there. It's total
peace and quiet where no one makes any demands.

—Judy, 58, New York, NY
(psychotherapist/psychoanalyst)

I get comfort by going to my mother's graveside and talking with her spirit. It works for me.

—Anonymous

There's a brook next to my house that's been my friend for many years. She provided me a place to play as a child and a place to reflect as a young adult. I can hear her from my room, so I open my window just a crack to listen to her comforting call. This helps me sleep when I'm troubled and relaxes me when I'm uptight.

—Valerie, 24, Washington, DC
(social worker/assistant crew coach)

I love going into the dance studio. The bare floors, sparse and simple surroundings just put me in a creative mood. I feel dance and movement are the most effective way to express all the deep emotions that I feel inside. When I dance I am fully in the moment and can let go of my daily stresses and responsibilities.

—Kelly, 34, Monmouth Bay, NJ
(acupuncturist)

Every Friday evening my wife and I try a different restaurant for dinner. We're both relaxed, the week's work has ended and we have the time and the opportunity to just sit and talk…and that's comforting.

—Fred, 60, New York, NY
(psychologist)

I go to an art class where I'm completely focused, so into what I'm doing I can't think of anything else. There's also a social component where people are pleasant and friendly; an easy camaraderie, which is a comfort.

—Christine, 58, New York, NY
(college administrator)

I find a sense of place, solitude and grounding in a library setting. I am able to quiet my insides and bring a sense of purpose and focus into my life. I remember weekly visits to the neighborhood library with my dad in Rochester. It gave me a feeling of specialness to accompany him.

—Marcia, 51, Fairlawn, NJ
(clinical social worker)

For many years on or around my birthday I'd surprise myself and go to the airport and quickly decide what places I could go to for a long weekend. I went to New Orleans to listen to jazz, another year to Chicago to attend a blues-jazz festival, and another time to Santa Fe for the opera. It was spur of the moment. I'd see what I felt like. I'd get a hotel room when I reached my destination. I treated myself to complete immersion in a new environment with new discoveries. It's been a lot of fun.

—Debbie, 48, Stamford, CT
(psychotherapist)

I have always thought of myself as a person who needs to get to the country, out of the city, for comfort. My initial impulse is to withdraw completely from the noise and bustle of the city, get to the light, quiet sereneness of my beloved Cape Cod—the ocean, the bay, the ponds. They will take care of me. I also think of other places where I have found solace—the Lincoln Mountains outside of Cloudcroft, New Mexico; Lolo Pass on the Idaho–Washington border; and a cove in Bolinas, California.

—Nancy, 59, New York, NY
(psychotherapist/gardener)

I fantasize about exotic vacations I'd like to take—a safari in Africa, skiing in the Alps, Thailand, India, Portugal and the Greek Islands. I like doing the homework: reading about the destination, planning what I'd see, where I'd stay, what restaurants I'd try. I'll even go to the library and take out some videos. This is enormous fun and gives me great satisfaction. Someday I'll go to these places and I'll be ready.

—Max, 21, Cleveland, OH
(cook)

The ocean. Clearly, there's something about the motion of the waves and the smell of salt air (plus the taste on your lips) that goes very deep in terms of primal comfort. Some people love the ocean in the fall, but my ideal is a warm summer day, with plenty of sun and a gentle breeze. Not only are there memories of childhood, with no responsibility and the sense of possibility, but even today being at the beach pushes problems away. There's a real sense of physical pleasure.

—Susan, 57, New York, NY
(retired advertising executive)

I sit on the floor of my husband's closet and smell his shirts. It's been months since 9/11, since his death, but sitting in his closet allows me to be with him, with his essence. His basketball, baseball bat, golf clubs, all of him is here. It's a small comfort.

—MaryAnne, 31, Staten Island, NY

There is nothing more comforting to me than sitting by the water. The ocean is my first choice, but since there is no ocean in East Kansas, any lake, pond, creek or river will do. So much the better if it's just rained. The noise that moving water makes, whether it's high-tide waves or just tired little lake ripples at sundown, blocks out the noise in my head. The sight of it rocking, falling, flickering, swelling to catch the wind, helps me to be still.

—Pat, 48, Lenexa, KS
(creative director)

Going to the gym builds up my self-esteem and allows me to vent my aggressive feeling.

—Cynthia, 38, New York, NY
(activist/school coordinator)

I am deeply comforted being at a religious liturgical celebration with beautiful music, gesture and preaching of the word of God. This always restores my faith, joy and energy.

—Edith, 62, Bronx, NY
(art conservationist)

Sun and sea. To be on the beach looking at the sea, the sun and the sky—how can anything be bad?

—Lois, 62, New York, NY
(social worker, grandmother)

My Comfort Places

_____

_____

_____

_____

_____

_____

_____

_____

_____

_____

If I had

but two loaves of bread,

I would sell one

and buy hyacinths,

for they would feed my soul.

—*Anonymous*

Things

I love flowers: in gardens, parks, nurseries, supermarkets, cut, put in pots, displayed in vases. I get comfort looking at them, smelling them, watching them grow. My favorites are paper whites, lilacs, stargazers, roses and gardenias.

—Lucie, 77, Berkeley, CA
(volunteer executive director)

The Saturday after 9/11 I went to a department store and bought new silk sheets, down pillows and a fabulous comforter. Then I went to the florist and bought potted flowers and two ficus trees. I never shopped so fast in my life. I'd wanted these particular things but kept putting off their purchase. No time. No money. Blah, blah, blah. What the hell. They jazz up the house. I feel great!

—Marilyn, 52, Fort Lee, NJ
(college professor)

I keep a number of scented candles in my kitchen cabinet for when I need down time. I've read that vanilla and green apple aromas are effective for reducing stress and anxiety.

—Sarah, 72, Miami, FL
(grandmother)

I always have a coloring book and crayons on hand. You'd be surprised how relaxing coloring is, no matter how old you are.

—Anonymous

My comfort clothes consist of high socks and a long velour robe that's been washed so many times it's like a second skin.

—Tina, 20, Hoboken, NJ
(secretary)

Waking up to the sound of church bells. It makes me feel that all is well with the world, even when it isn't.

—Marie, 58, Santa Monica, CA
(actress/writer/producer/editor/teacher/work-in-progress)

I keep a daily journal and each day list three things that made me happy and/or three things I accomplished (i.e. went for a walk; got a manicure; sent a get-well card, etc.). This puts me in a positive frame of mind and I can look back and see I've taken care of business...and of myself.

—Lydia, 29, Richmond, VA

I have a set of watercolors and a sketch pad I bought in the arts and crafts store. Sometimes when I feel bored or preoccupied, I let go on paper and allow the colors to lead me. I'm always fascinated by the end product.

—Beth, 30, Denver, CO

After 9/11 I wanted to give presents to the people in my life. I wanted them to know how grateful I was for their love and support. And I wanted them to know I believed that we all had a future. I gave my mom, sisters, aunt, uncle and best friend subscriptions to magazines. It felt good to be able to give.

—Jack, 30, Short Hills, NJ

Whenever I go on a trip, I buy postcards of the sights I've seen. Instead of sending them, I take them home and pin them to a bulletin board I keep in the kitchen. When I'm down I just look at these cards and remember the sense of joy and adventure I felt in those distant cities.

—Betty, 47, Great Neck, NY
(teacher)

I love a thick, soft, white, spa-style robe wrapped around me. I feel like it can protect me from anything bad. Also, it feels luxurious and extravagant.

—Phoebe, 24, New York, NY
(graduate student)

When I was in the hospital for a few days, a friend brought me a teddy bear. I felt so vulnerable during that time. The bear gave me courage and comfort. I slept with him, sat up with him on my lap. I'm an adult but this was the very best present. Now, he sits watching over me from my bookcase at home.

—Joyce, 39, San Francisco, CA
(saleswoman)

THINGS

A friend gave me a whistle right before 9/11 to use when I go running. It now gives me great comfort. I know I won't be alone if I'm in a threatening situation. I know someone will hear my call for help.

—George, 62, New York, NY
(retired banker)

A cheap treat. I'll buy six helium balloons and tie them to the two lamps and one chair in my bedroom. Sometimes I'll do one color, like all purple, or I'll choose a group of pastels during the dark winter months. I walk into my bedroom…and I smile…and feel happy.

—Helaine, 32, Lancaster, PA
(graduate student)

The first thing I did after 9/11 was to buy a small pocket flashlight for my purse. Being prepared and organized makes me feel better, more in control. If I'm feeling in control, if I've taken care of my well-being, then I'm comforted.

—Rose, 61, Roslyn, NY
(volunteer)

Yes, I have a blankie…sort of. Growing up, I was very close to my grandma. When she got sick and was put in a nursing home almost ten years ago I made a point of claiming the huge cream-colored comforter she had on her bed for years. I couldn't tell her how much it meant to me because her illness had progressed to the point where she forgot who I was. But whenever I'm sick, watching television, knitting, or reading, I take that huge comforter and wrap it around me. It's weird, but I use it in the summer and in the winter, and I'm never too hot or too cold. Just right. And although it's been washed a dozen times, it still smells a little bit like her house. It's as close to her as I can get these days since she passed away in 1994.

—Aminda, 25, Ridgefield Park, NJ
(graduate student)

My Sunday shirt brings me comfort. It's a polo type but the fabric design is a little funky. I don't wear it when I'm going out, so unconsciously I began to wear it when I got home from church on Sunday when I knew I wasn't going anywhere. I knew I was going to sit and watch the final round of whatever golf match was being played that week. My wife likes to watch with me, but she reads the paper and naps on the couch next to me at the same time. When it's over we go to the kitchen and make dinner, usually together.

—Warren, 40, New York, NY
(stage technician)

I work in downtown Manhattan and was incredibly grateful to be alive after 9/11. A week later I just decided to put up the Christmas lights…in my kitchen. They're still up. I don't know when I'll take them down. For now, there's something hopeful about the little lights.

—Will, 33, Bayside, NY
(stockbroker)

Crossword puzzles. What a comfort! I forget about everything when I do them. I also keep writing journals. It's a great way to express myself, to sort out feelings, to problem-solve.

—Daralee, 66, New York, NY
(college teacher)

My teddy bear collection began when I became principal of a primary school. I purchased a bear (Ralph) in a bag. His eyes just popped over the top of the bag. When the children came into my office it was a great talking point. Some children gave me some small bears to keep Ralph company. When I left the school, the community presented me with a rather large bear—John. And there have been others; all remind me of the special people who gave them to me, so sometimes I sit and hug them and remember those people and that is very comforting.

—Colin, 50, Victoria, Australia
(teacher, small-business mentor)

I remember as a very young child hiding under a table in the living room that was covered with a beautiful hand-crocheted lace tablecloth. Sometimes my mother would lift a corner of the cloth, peek under and say, "There you are!" Other times she would just let me stay there. As an adult I've discovered I love lace. I love to follow the patterns and curves of the lines and spaces. Whenever I walk the beach, preferably in early morning or at sunset, I look for lace. There's a point when the tide comes in and then recedes. It leaves tiny ripples moving back from the shore—images of lace wonderfully glistening, different each time. The soft bubbles breaking into holes on the sand—lace. Blankets of it. I find this so exciting, comforting, and rejuvenating.

—Andrea, 57, New York, NY
(learner)

I covered the shelves in my refrigerator with lace doilies. Every time I open the door, the sight of them makes me smile.

—Anna, 82, Miami, FL
(ballroom dancer)

I like using my wonderful magic-wand vibrator. It's quick, easy, delicious, a pick-me-up, relaxes my muscles, energizes my brain, gives a quicker step to my walk. I do this whenever possible and without fanfare.

—Ruth, 54, Bronx, NY
(psychotherapist)

Wrapping myself in my warm blue "Afghan" blanket is a comfort. This well-worn blanket and a long-gone twin were used by my father and me when watching TV. Perhaps we were cold, perhaps not, but we were rarely without our blankets. My memories of my father are not usually filled with warmth, so it is a wonder to me even now that I find such comfort in an item treasured equally by him.

—Alan, 55, New York, NY
(college administrator)

National Geographic magazine transports me to other worlds and has such beautiful photography.

—Cathy, 39, Salisbury, CT
(photographer)

Lying in bed on flannel sheets and pillowcases provides me with the most comforting, cuddliest, cozy sleep possible.

—Carol, 41, Pittsburgh, PA
(lawyer)

THINGS

Flowers by the bed always—total life experience of wellness and calm.

—Debbie, 53, New York, NY
(registered nurse)

My Comfort Things

_____

_____

_____

_____

_____

_____

_____

_____

_____

_____

To learn respect and reverence for process is

what counts.

We each take our own roads, but it is what

one discovers along that road

that's important, and how one is changed by

those discoveries.

—Judith Guest
(author)

Movies/Videos

My favorite movie is Jacques Tati's *Mr. Hulot's Holiday*, a French film from 1953. I think I was twenty years old when I first saw it. The synopsis: "When a well-intentioned nit-wit spends his vacation at a seaside resort, he gets involved in one hilarious incident after another. In addition to many comic mishaps, affectionately drawn caricatures poignantly reveal that side of our own human nature which wants to have fun—no matter what." I own two copies of this video. Every time I see it, it takes me back to the simpler summer days of the 1950s. It makes me feel good and relaxes me. I feel as if I've had a summer vacation no matter what the season.

—**George, 62, New York, NY
(retired banker)**

Shall We Dance is a delightful Japanese film (subtitles) where learning something new, perseverance, commitment and trust pay off. I've seen it four times and it continues to leave me with hope and a sense of renewal.

—Betty, 47, Great Neck, NY
(teacher)

I love watching *Rocky* with Sylvester Stallone because it gives me a sense of hope and motivates me to overcome even the toughest obstacles.

—Jose, 20, New York, NY
(student)

Walking and Talking is a wonderful film about friendship between women. The two protagonists have been best friends since childhood and the film explores what happens to their relationship when one of them announces she's getting married. I've actually referred to this movie as my comfort movie for the ages.

—Susanna, 39, New York, NY
(graduate student)

The video *Breaking Away* inspires me to go after my goals. The young men persevere and triumph although no one believes they will. That's comforting to think of when I'm in a tough situation.

—Ben, 39, Boston, MA
(travel agent)

I love *Top Hat* and any of the *Thin Man* series of films. The characters in all of them are dapper, the settings range from glamorous deco to grungy criminal lairs. The plots are easy to understand and to get lost in. (The latter is most important to me.)

—Pat, 55, New York, NY
(psychologist/analyst)

Comfort is watching a movie with a happy ending. Two good examples for me are: *The Princess Bride* (directed by Rob Reiner, starring Robin Wright, Mandy Patinkin, Christopher Guest and Peter Falk) and *Parenthood* (directed by Ron Howard, starring Steve Martin).

—Jeff, 38, Brooklyn, NY
(attorney/woodworker)

In terms of film I am most comforted by the works of the late Soviet filmmaker Andrei Tarkovsky. He only made seven films in his lifetime, but each is an extension of some permanent human theme that we, as a young nation, tend to forget. Themes of place, home and sanctuary; remembrance and nostalgia, sacrifice, humility, forgiveness and suffering; silence, prayer and redemption. The films of Tarkovsky remind me that I'm a thinking, feeling, wondering, poetic being worthy of considering life in the deepest ways possible and not just as an amused consumer drone.

—Ed, 51, Norwood, MA
(English and film teacher)

When I'm feeling down I'll pull out the old Doris Day/Rock Hudson movie *Pillow Talk*. For whatever reason this never fails to make me laugh.

—Joan, 59, St. Louis, MO
(gerontologist/writer)

I love watching *Ruby in Paradise*, a 1993 film directed by Victor Nuñez and starring Ashley Judd. This is a lovely story of a young woman who leaves home and finds her own way despite hardship. Empowering.

—Cathy, 39, Salisbury, CT
(photographer)

Whenever I watch *Singin' in the Rain*, the two scenes that put a smile on my face are "Gotta Dance" and Gene Kelly doing the title song. I can't keep myself from singing and dancing around my room.

—Susan, 55, New York, NY
(program director)

I love Victor Borge videos; a lot of beautiful music and comedy. He's lifted me out of darkness many, many times.

—Diana, 50, New York, NY
(musician/mom)

The Piano with Holly Hunter is a visual orgasm. The story, set in nineteenth-century New Zealand, is hauntingly, cinematically gorgeous. I love every single beautiful image.

—Paul, 37, New York, NY
(makeup artist)

My favorite movie is *To Kill a Mockingbird*, based on Harper Lee's best-selling novel. I love the time period and the Southern small-town atmosphere. The kids are awesome and Gregory Peck as the father/lawyer is amazing; a caring, loving presence.

—Christine, 49, New York, NY
(social worker)

A surefire way for me to feel better is to watch *Moonstruck*, starring Cher and Nicolas Cage. The movie is about complex relationships and trying to work them out when there's conflict and imperfection, and thinking one has to compromise but ultimately being willing to try again and following your heart.

—Naomi, 48, New York, NY
(psychoanalyst)

A comfort movie for me is *Amadeus*, where Mozart's ability to create is not constrained by his physical limitations.

—Dale, 63, Venice, CA
(filmmaker/writer)

Silent films with live music make my blues melt away. I program a silent film series featuring either a solo pianist or a quintet and larger groupings if possible. Music in film started as a means of masking the noisy projector. It wasn't long before the music started to make some sense with what was happening on the screen. I spend Wednesday evenings watching classics, comedies, dramas, mysteries, etc., with a full audience booing and hissing the villains and heroes/heroines on the screen while encouraging the musicians along. It's possible to rent good silents from the homespun video dealers vs. the big boys.

—**Ray, 37, Boulder, CO**
(concert promoter)

My favorite movie is *Blazing Saddles*, directed by Mel Brooks. I used to watch this movie every day for months. It's irreverent, silly and outrageous. I originally saw it with my father and we both laughed so hard we cried. The dialogue between Gene Wilder and Cleavon Little is priceless. This movie never fails to lift my spirits. Enjoy!

—**Bodden, Elmsford, NY**
(assistant director of training)

My Comfort Movies/Videos

_____

_____

_____

_____

_____

_____

_____

_____

_____

_____

Every child is an artist;

the problem is

how to remain an artist

once you grow up.

—Pablo Picasso
(artist)

Inside Activities

For the past couple of years I've used the last Sunday of the month just for me. I stay in bed the whole day. I don't answer the phone. I catch up on reading the magazines I've saved. I call out for food to be delivered. I don't get out of my robe. I just hang out with myself. This time-out restores my strength and energy.

—Lauren, 48, Denver, CO
(accountant)

I like to decorate my apartment. Fixing or attempting to fix things around my house by myself makes me feel proud if I can do it, and if I can't, finding out how I can fix it makes me feel good about myself.

—Jazmin, 27, Bronx, NY
(legal advocate)

I play Scrabble with my husband. I love the competition and the fun we have together.

—Lee, 60+, Bayside, NY
(retired)

I write all my feelings, thoughts and ideas in my daily journal. This helps me remember what I felt like when I was going through something difficult or my frame of mind at a certain time.

—Anonymous

I engage in handicrafts. For me, making dolls helps me stay focused. It also adds to my sense of accomplishment when it's done.

—Anna, Brooklyn, NY

I find some quiet time where I can sit down and pick up my favorite craft, quilting. It seems when my hands are busy my mind doesn't wander and dwell on the troubles/concerns of the day.

—Anonymous

Watching a baseball game on TV is very comforting because it's ritualistic, rhythmic and has a stately pace. It reminds me of the connection I have with my dad.

—Jan, 51, Cottonwood, AZ
(counselor)

In the past few years, on Sunday afternoons at around 3:00, I've gone to some musical concerts in churches. This practice provides me with a welcome but unexpected comfort zone. Kids fully engaged in homework, husband contentedly prostrate in front of the televised football, weekend tasks and socialization completed, dinner still several hours away—I take off for motets, fugues and cantatas. I'm cared for by the strains of a quartet, pianist or choir. I can sit quietly among strangers and have my very being caressed by the strains of the music surrounding me and reverberating off the marble walls and arches. A few hours later I am refreshed, stilled, comforted and can approach the new week more openly.

—Nancy, 59, New York, NY
(psychotherapist/gardener)

Salsa dancing. I feel very happy and content and appreciated and grateful that men and women with nothing else
in common can get together and give each other pleasure
and laughs in this way. Sooooooo fun! Pure ultra pleasure.

—Sheila, 44, New York, NY
(writer)

I try to have friends in on a regular basis for a potluck
supper. I'll assign main dishes, salads, and desserts. We'll
spend the evening trading stories, experiences and ideas.
It's always comforting, always energizing.

—Jennifer, 33, Montclair, NJ
(jewelry designer)

I take a fifteen- or thirty-minute tea break. I just sit in
one comfortable place that's relaxing and actually drink a
whole cup of tea slowly and thoughtfully without getting
up to do anything for anyone else. It's hard at first not to
be compelled to straighten things up, but I don't. Being
still is a learned skill, but it's been very beneficial.

—Marina, 40, Natick, MA
(partner, crafts gallery)

I light a candle in a dark room and burn some incense and let my mind roam free. It lets me put into focus my life and loves. It also lets me recharge my psychic batteries so I can face the next day with all my energy.

—Frank, 35, New York, NY
(human resources administrator)

Going through family photo albums with my wife and daughter is a comfort. Although my daughter is now a young adult (arrghh!), I am easily transported back in time to her early childhood as we turn the pages of our first family albums. I see pictures of my infant daughter sleeping on my chest; a toddler grappling with a peach or smeared in chocolate; and a young child playing with a cousin at the beach or in animated and intimate conversation with a friend. My heart feels a pang as I remember those innocent days, which—though they will never return—somehow survived adolescence and provide the foundation for the honest and loving relationship that exists today.

—Alan, 55, New York, NY
(college administrator)

What a joy to wrap myself in a big fluffy quilt, drink a cup of hot chocolate on a cold winter's afternoon, and just daydream.

—Erika, 28, Bronx, NY
(office superwoman)

I like doing craft projects, making things for others and then seeing the happy look on their faces when I give them a gift.

—Petra, 50, Bronx, NY
(teacher)

I watch football on TV. The sounds of the game, the memories of being at a stadium, the excitement and the pageantry are all really soothing to me. Sometimes I write in the next room with the sounds on. Sometimes I nap. I eat cheese and crackers and maybe chili. And I call my mom, who is inevitably watching the game too, and crow about a turnover, a touchdown or an amazing play. I like college better than pro, but I am content to watch either.

—Gillian, 30, Iowa City, IA
(poet, jester)

I work on the pottery wheel. It's completely relaxing, childlike and creative, and channels any stressful or negative feelings into positive ones.

—Anonymous

Cooking is comforting—soups, stews, baking. It makes me feel useful and important and reminds me of my grandmother's farm kitchen with a huge range, soft sofa, cats on the outside window ledge waiting to be fed, miles of Yorkshire countryside between us and the real world. Cooking leads into having friends round, which always makes me feel better, too.

—Stephanie, 44, London, England
(writer)

Zen meditation is a comfort. I sit on a burgundy cushion against a black pillow, quieting my mind. I hear the silence all around me. I gaze gently at the beautiful yellow wooden floor, the scent of incense all around, and know in my heart I'm home, I'm safe, I'm exactly where I want to be.

—Ruth, 54, Bronx, NY
(psychotherapist)

Needlepoint keeps me busy. I focus my mind on the activity instead of running a hundred miles a minute in my brain.

—Nicki, 32, Muttontown, NY
(mother)

From mid-November through mid-January I grow/force amaryllis bulbs. I like to buy them at different stages of growth (early bud, 4 inches tall, etc.) to stagger the flowering. I'll also buy a variety of colors: pink, red, candy-striped and white. Each day there's new growth, new activity in the pots. I love just happening upon them when I open the door to my house.

—Marilyn, 52, Fort Lee, NJ
(college professor)

Comfort is practicing/sparring at Hapkido (Korean martial art), because it releases my negative energy and restores my positive energy while increasing my self-defense skills.

—Victoria, 32, New York, NY
(researcher)

I do a fair amount of woodworking and remodeling. When I'm working in my shop, I get a feeling of accomplishment that comes from making something I have complete control over. When working with clients, I'm creative, but always bound to the constraints of their needs. The woodworking is just for me.

**—Rich, 35, Highland, IN
(graphic designer)**

I'm a Buddhist and meditate to center and rejuvenate my life energy and bring clarity and peace to my mental processes. I meditate twice a day (usually), morning and evening, in a personal Buddhist service in a special place set up in my home.

**—Eric, 56, West Los Angeles, CA
(financial planner, father/husband/seeker—
not necessarily in that order)**

Comfort is spending a Sunday snoozing and making love to my wife.

**—Michael, 71, Oakland, CA
(retired)**

Watching wrestling, the World Wrestling Federation [now World Wrestling Entertainment] and Big Japan hard-core, makes me happy. I'd like to pursue this at some time and talking about it motivates me.

—Danny, 22, Bronx, NY
(comedian)

Comfort is going home. It's loving where I live. It's closing the door of my apartment and knowing I don't have to put on a "happy face" or be in a good mood or stay one minute longer in my business suit.

—Trudy, 45, Chicago, IL
(stockbroker)

I save the greeting cards, birthday cards and notes that friends send me in a box I keep under my bed. When I'm feeling blue I'll sort through the cards. It makes me feel better to re-read the messages.

—Phyllis, 29, Queens, NY
(waitress)

I find taking a hot bath in Epsom salts very comforting.
Hot baths are soothing and relaxing and relieve my body
of tension. In the water I spontaneously begin thinking
about pleasant things.

—Lenwood, 53, Brooklyn, NY
(occupational therapist)

I've lately gotten involved with board-game parties. I've
roped in five friends and we meet once a week at someone's house. We order take-out for dinner so there's no
mess and for four to five hours we'll play Scrabble,
Monopoly, Pictionary, even bingo. A great way to get
together. Good talk. Wonderful fun!

—Lilly, 39, Philadelphia, PA
(decorator)

My Comfort Inside Activities

_____

_____

_____

_____

_____

_____

_____

_____

_____

_____

In three words I can sum up everything

I've learned about life:

It goes on.

—Robert Frost
(poet)

Outside Activities

When I'm hiking, life is simplified. My concerns are food, water, shelter and reaching my destination. This simplicity combined with beautiful surroundings gives me peace.

—Anonymous

I enjoy riding the bus and watching the parents who are truly enjoying their young children—playing with them, laughing with them, hugging and kissing them, reading them stories or answering their questions. When this happens, people on the bus are smiling and I think we all feel the world is a happier place.

—Louise, 56, New York, NY
(social worker)

Swimming. The movement in the water makes me feel a oneness with the universe. I feel spiritual and calm.

—Barbara, 56, Brooklyn, NY

Being outside—almost anyplace, anytime—reminds me that my body was not created to sit behind a desk.

—Nicolas, 36, Waltham, MA
(president of own firm)

I go to the creek and find a small stone, hold it in my hand and talk/pray about what's on my mind. I send all of this into the stone in my hand, and when I'm done I throw the stone into the water and let the water carry the pain away.

—Jan, 51, Cottonwood, AZ
(counselor)

I'm a hands-on person. I need to see the end product. So working on my car, making it better, allows me to get distance from my problems. I see the results of my hard work and I feel all right.

—Ralph, 50, Bronx, NY
(dad)

I like to play baseball. It works out my aggression after a long, hard day. It's good fun, sweaty, comforting.

—Cynthia, Cottonwood, AZ

Cutting and splitting firewood (particularly if it begins with felling a tree) is pleasurable because overall it gives me a great sense of accomplishment. But to be more specific, I enjoy the strenuous exercise it requires, the sense of tension or danger involved with using a chainsaw and dropping a tree (without personal injury, of course), the feel of the maul (the ax) when the cut-up logs split and the smell of the wood. Finally, after an afternoon's work, I can look at the stacked wood and feel good that I have produced something that my wife and I will enjoy in a year or two when the firewood has dried. It is one of my few activities that has immediate, tangible and visible results.

—John, 56, New York, NY
(banker/dream: to retire comfortably)

I go for a bike ride in the park so I can feel more connected with nature and with my body.

—Anna, Brooklyn, NY

Shopping is a comfort. I grew up shopping with my mother. I can't think of any of her clothes in my entire memory that I didn't help her shop for. As an adult we would combine shopping with lunch or dinner out and talk. Now that my mother can no longer shop, the activity reminds me of her, makes me feel close to her in some way.

—Mary, 53, New York, NY
(health care administrator)

Walking makes me feel connected. I feel as though I'm accomplishing something–getting exercise, seeing new sights and appreciating my time instead of whiling it away. Paying attention, I get to see people being themselves in different situations, and I can compare my own reactions in similar situations, or contemplate how their reactions make me feel. Lastly, isolation is a very inward-focused state, but being out and about is more outward-focused–think of it as the difference between watching a movie based on a true story and being in the story itself.

—Jeff, 38, Brooklyn, NY
(attorney/woodworker)

It comforts me to walk. Mere motion without any particular destination or incentive shouldn't be so satisfying, but it is. And quite often serendipitous, spirit-raising sightings just occur, if one is paying attention at all. Walking in New York City is a particular joy, and I love playing the game of following the WALK lights (following the WALK light at any corner and letting it lead you on) to discover areas of Manhattan I'd never seen before. I also love (in NYC) doing second-story walks, i.e. paying attention to what lies above the immediate street view.

—Jeff, 56, Cold Spring, NY
(writer)

Getting in my van and driving around gives me time to think. I'll talk to myself and to my brother and father, who are in heaven.

—Anonymous

When I feel anxious or have the need to move, Rollerblading makes me feel energized and forceful.

—Christopher, 13, Bronx, NY
(student)

Riding my motorcycle is a way to get away. Just me. It also gives me a connection to the road that the car does not allow. Temperature is felt, wind is perceived, turns are anticipated and leaned into. It removes me from the distractions of the mundane world.

—Creighton, 34, San Diego, CA

I'm a pilot and enjoy flying. Since this is potentially dangerous, everything else when I'm in the air (work, family, relationships) becomes secondary. I clear my mind and concentrate only on the flying. The sense of accomplishment and feeling of relaxation lasts, for me, a full day after my flight.

—Andrew, 32, New York, NY
(broadcast journalist)

Going jogging is when I meditate. Insights about specific problems come to me at this time. Maybe it's being in nature or concentrating on my breathing, but I usually feel more connected after a run.

—Kenneth, 43, Brooklyn, NY
(counselor)

I have always found the garden a great place to relieve stress. I've recently retired from a job in sales that required a lot of travel as well as constant deadlines, and to be outside in fresh air (vs. canned office air) has always been a huge release. Pulling weeds allows me to let go of a great deal of frustration, and at the end of the day I've actually accomplished something!

—**Kathleen, 51, Pawling, NY
(retired)**

During the spring, if I'm depressed, a walk in the rain without an umbrella is good for cleansing the spirit and soul. I get to think of all the possibilities that I have in life. Why worry about this one when the world is out there for the taking?

—**Frank, 35, New York, NY
(human resources administrator)**

When I'm frustrated, the physical challenges from bike riding–pushing up a hill–can jump my motor up a level and switch off stress and fatigue.

—**Bob, 51, Pompton Plains, NJ
(horseshoer)**

Every time I go fly-fishing I learn something new and that keeps me interested. There's a lot going on, the timing of the cast, the drift, the strike, the fight, the landing of the fish, the release, all have their part. I find it comforting and relaxing to be standing in the river, surveying what's been given to me, and being able to see the trout's behavior, get in tune and hopefully catch a few. I release everything I catch. I like to go with one friend, but will gladly go alone too. Solitude on the river is easy. I tie my own flies at home before I go, so that's part of the relaxation for me. I never thought I'd be this interested in bugs! I just enjoy being out in nature, without disturbing it too much. I use barbless flies, so I can unhook a fish quickly, with no damage. Sometimes it's the hike to get there; sometimes it's the sunset or sunrise while there. Sometimes it's the birds that I see, or just a nice day off from work. It's worth every minute that I spend to do it.

—Matt, 33, Boulder, CO
(sales rep)

Playing golf brings me both comfort and agony. You're out in the open air, usually with friends. You're playing well and this brings delight because it's a very hard game. When you hit a great shot your friends congratulate you because they understand the difficulty. When you hit a bad shot your friends usually don't say anything. They know you're upset. If they do say something, it's about how you got a bad break, or something that puts some of the blame on the golf course. In the end you've spent four to five hours with friends, trying to conquer the golf course, and if you've finished, in a way, you've won.

—Warren, 40, New York, NY
(stage technician)

My Comfort Outside Activities

_____

_____

_____

_____

_____

_____

_____

_____

_____

_____

Sorrow shared is halved

And joy shared

Is doubled.

—Native American saying

Quotations

"After this I shall think nothing of falling downstairs."

This quote is from *Alice in Wonderland* by Lewis Carroll. It gives me a feeling of having overcome a very challenging situation.

—Susan, 51, Lawrence, MA
(realtor)

The late actress Ruth Gordon wrote:

"When I'm sad the first thing I do is clean out my sock drawer."

I've taken the advice. I straighten, organize and clean, while remembering, discarding, accepting. That was then, this is now. Begin again.

—Jane, Richmond, VA
(friend)

My favorite quote is by Johann Wolfgang von Goethe and it offers me hope:

"Whatever you can do or dream you can begin it; Boldness has genius, power and magic in it."

—Nilda, 46, New York, NY
(legal advocate)

Eleanor Roosevelt said:

"You gain strength and confidence by every experience in which you really stop to look fear in the face. You must do the thing you think you cannot do."

And so I try.

—Rose, 61, Roslyn, NY
(volunteer)

An important quote for me is by Emile Zola:

"What did you come here to do? I came to live out loud."

Living out loud has become a mantra. For me it means to stay present, stay solid, stay honest.

—Jane, 57, New York, NY
(psychotherapist/writer)

After my husband died I found a plaque that says:

"Hope and keep busy."

The quote is from *Little Women,* and looking at it always helps me keep going a little longer when I think I can't. It's such simple advice but it makes such good sense.

—**Sharon, 55, Lawrence, MA
(children's activities director)**

I say the Serenity Prayer once a day and this gives me strength.

"God grant me the serenity to accept the things I cannot change, courage to change the things I can and the wisdom to know the difference."

—**Ben, 39, Boston, MA
(travel agent)**

I read this quote by the actress Gwyneth Paltrow:

"The best way to mend a broken heart is time and girlfriends."

And I thought, yes!

—**Phyllis, 29, Queens, NY
(waitress)**

My favorite thought is:

"Stressed spelled backwards is desserts."

What a perfect antidote. How cool is that?!

—Harry, 48, Westchester, NY
(carpenter)

When I'm struggling with my weight I try to remember this thought by the sculptor Brancusi:

"The human body is beautiful only insofar as it mirrors the soul."

—Lilly, 39, Philadelphia, PA
(decorator)

"Perfectionism is self-abuse of the highest order." —psychologist Anne Wilson Schaef

I keep this sign over my desk. It seems to keep me in check and slow me down. Then I say to myself as a reminder: "Knock it off. Just let yourself be."

—Helaine, 32, Lancaster, PA
(graduate student)

This quote by the author Harriet Beecher Stowe always keeps me on my toes:

"One part of the science of living is to learn just what our responsibility is, and to let other people's alone."

—Lauren, 48, Denver, CO
(accountant)

On a Post-it on my mirror, to give me courage each morning, is this advice from the educator Marva Collins:

"Trust yourself. Think for yourself. Act for yourself. Speak for yourself. Be yourself. Imitation is suicide."

—Sophie, 72, Miami, FL
(grandmother)

When I feel like doing some emotional eating, when food appears to be the answer but I know it's really not, I get brought back to earth (sometimes) by a quote from Julia Child:

"Life itself is the proper binge."

—Judy, 29, Freeport, NY
(bookstore clerk)

Kathy Kendall. I don't know who she is or what she's done. But I do know I love her quote and repeat it to myself on a frequent basis.

"I have to tell the negative committee that meets in my head to sit down and shut up."

—**Anonymous**

"The aim of life is to live, and to live means to be aware, joyously, drunkenly, serenely, divinely aware."–author Henry Miller

I take this as a challenge. An exhortation to really "go for it!" I carry the saying in my wallet and it gives me that extra dose of courage.

—**Frank, 36, Columbia, MD**
(artist)

Elisabeth Kübler-Ross, a physician and spiritual healer, has taught me many things through her writings and her life. This quote of hers gives me comfort:

"Learn to get in touch with the silence within yourself and know that everything in this life has a purpose."

—**Trudy, 45, Chicago, IL**
(stockbroker)

QUOTATIONS

I love this quote by Louis Armstrong—as straight to the heart as he played his trumpet.

"I got a simple rule about everybody. If you don't treat me right—shame on you."

—Helen, 59, Chicago, IL
(retired)

The quotation:

"What doesn't kill you makes you stronger"

comforts me with its optimistic focus on continuously getting better and stronger.

—Gary, 49, Manhattan Beach, CA
(investment adviser, parent of 3 teenagers)

I love the work of novelist Iris Murdoch. She died from Alzheimer's disease. The movie *Iris* is about her life. She once said:

"One of the secrets of a happy life is continuous small treats."

Makes sense, right? Just plain old good advice. Give to yourself on a regular basis.

—Walter, 42, Burlington, VT
(high school teacher/poet)

One of my favorite sayings is:

"Strength through softness."

When I'm stressed and feeling angry I try to think about being strong but silent, allowing myself to focus on that which I can control and not on the things I can't. I'll also write things down, allowing myself to distance from them, coming back when I've released some of my anger.

**—Bob, 46, Riverside, CA
(psychologist)**

The ideas/quotes: *"Everything works out for the best"* and *"If it's meant to be, it will be"* bring me comfort because they make me feel as if the outcome and/or course of events are out of my control. It's freeing to think I can't control the outcome of every situation. I'm willing to give in to destiny's fate.

—Anonymous

I'm encouraged by what Johann Sebastian Bach said:

"There's nothing remarkable about it. All one has to do is hit the right keys at the right time and the instrument plays itself."

He makes it seem like anyone can make music. And that anything's possible.

—Dennis, 31, Falls Church, VA
(drummer/dreamer)

My Comfort Quotations

_____

_____

_____

_____

_____

_____

_____

_____

_____

_____

Life is like music;

it must be composed by ear,

feeling and instinct,

not by rule.

—Samuel Butler
(poet/author)

Music

Playing the harmonica makes me feel happy because the sound is so sweet. I have a group of friends who think of me as a troubadour, which makes me feel appreciated.

**—Christopher, 13, Bronx, NY
(student)**

I like to listen to soft piano music. George Winston has some beautiful albums such as *Autumn* and *December*. His music makes me really feel those seasons.

—Anonymous

The song "I Will Survive" by Gloria Gaynor is empowering. The lyrics have served me well through many a difficult time.

—Anonymous

There's something about the ripeness and virtuosity of the opera singer Marilyn Horne's voice. It is so riveting and pleasurable that listening to her creates an almost physical sense of enjoyment. It must be kind of like an addictive drug, because there are some passages I feel compelled to play over and over again. I find myself going back to "Canzonetta Spagnuola," a song by Rossini. It's fun and upbeat and incredibly difficult to sing. Twice in the song she does something called *messa di voce* where she holds a note (this one very low in her incredible chest voice), makes it louder and softer, all without taking a breath. You've never heard anything like it.

—Susan, 57, New York, NY
(retired advertising executive)

I listen to Chanticleer's CD *Our Heart's Joy*. The sounds of this a cappella group, in particular the "Ave Maria," pierces my heart, dissolving my resistance to feeling and connects me to myself.

—Melissa, 48, New York, NY
(psychotherapist/healer)

Listening to some dig-in-deep-to-your-soul gospel music makes me feel good. I cry, I laugh, I dance, I get calm. It takes the pain away and I realize I am never alone. I especially love the CD *Great Women of Gospel Volume II*.

—Juanita, 42, New York, NY
(counselor)

What comforts me at the moment is Ani DiFranco's CD *Dilate*. I always listen to this album when I'm really hurt or angry because all of the songs are very charged and emotional. She has so many "angry" songs where she sings to the person that pissed her off and gets to say all the things that I wish I could say. So in that light I find it to be a very cathartic, empowering album.

—Karin, 19, New York, NY
(student/waitress/actress)

When I'm happy and comfortable in myself, showtunes will pop out of my mouth. I'll sing songs from *The Sound of Music*, *West Side Story*, *My Fair Lady*, *Bells Are Ringing* and *A Chorus Line*.

—Beth, 55, Miami, FL
(painter)

I like hearing Stevie Wonder's *Songs in the Key of Life* and *Original Musiquarium 1*. Both are wonderful compilations that make me sing and dance. Los Lobos' *Kiko* is a soulful, catchy and complex collection of tunes that I also find quite lovely.

—Anonymous

Faintly silly songs like "Shiny Happy People" (R.E.M.), "Something in the Air" (Thunderclap Newman) and "Delilah" (Tom Jones) make me laugh and sing along. There's also a cathartic purpose to sad/evocative music that gives me an excuse for a good cry. For instance, when I was in Manhattan on September 11, all I wanted to hear was "Born to Run" (Bruce Springsteen).

—Anonymous

"Send in the Clowns" is a beautiful song that makes me say I can do it no matter what. It's inspirational and says never give up. It always gives me hope.

—Hilda, 50, New York, NY
(activist)

Irish music touches something in my soul and plucks at my heartstrings. It brings back childhood memories…of evenings spent around the fireplace with my father telling tales of the banshees and the leprechauns. I love the CD *Now and in Time to Be*. It's a combination of music and poetry—W. B. Yeats reading his poems to music. I also enjoy a popular Irish band called the Chieftains. They have two wonderful CDs: *The Black Veil* and *Tears of Stone*. And in a rather irreverent modern style is the CD *Christy Moore at the Point Live*. Great fun!

—Therese, 68, New York, NY
(psychotherapist)

The Dave Brubeck CD *Time Out* is the only CD I have that is incomplete if you listen to any one song by itself. Every song is incredibly well written and flows into the song that comes before and after it. The only song that might stand by itself is "Take Five", but why would you listen to "Take Five" by itself when it sounds so much better coming after "Strange Meadow Lark"? The whole CD is complex but soothing. To me it feels like graceful simplicity.

—Warren, 40, New York, NY
(stage technician)

Learning to play an instrument got me through a period of unemployment. I had to work at something. I had to practice. I forgot myself when I was playing the flute. I had no talent but I got better. What a reward!

—Linda, 60, Washington, DC
(program analyst)

I like solitude and listening to Mozart's opera *The Magic Flute* and Chopin and Beethoven symphonies. In a different mood I like the old-timers like the Carpenters and Peter, Paul and Mary. Then for jazz it's Sarah Vaughan and Ella Fitzgerald singing Cole Porter.

—Barbara, 63, Norwalk, CT
(retired social worker)

For soothing music it's Loreena McKennitt's *The Visit* (Celtic, spiritual). I listen to Beth Hart's *Screamin' for My Supper*. She prevails after a tough journey. And then I like Tori Amos' *Little Earthquakes*—good for getting in touch with my anger.

—Cathy, 39, Salisbury, CT
(photographer)

In terms of music, I think the Beach Boys' *Pet Sounds* is one of the two or three most perfect inventions of the twentieth century (baseball, the Beatles and Calvin and Hobbes being some others). This record is a diary of Brian Wilson's own fragile adolescence and his musings on leaving home, growing up, returning home and struggling with change. *Pet Sounds* is a tender work which, after thirty-five years, still resonates with me in ways that engage my own memory of adolescence as a time when anything was possible, nothing was trivial, but authenticity was elusive. I am most comforted by this record because it makes me feel less alone in this world.

—**Ed, 51, Norwood, MA**
(English and film teacher)

When I'm upset I usually play the piano. I've been playing for about ten years now and when I play it calms me down, comforts me and makes me feel much better.

—**Christen, 53, Lawrence, MA**
(children's birthday party planner)

John Coltrane's *My Favorite Things*. I love popping in the CD and playing it at a loud volume. Sometimes I use it to turn around my mood, and sometimes it's used for some good wallowing.

—Peter, 31, Brooklyn, NY
(teacher)

Schubert's "Symphony no. 9" is so powerful and majestic it takes me away from dwelling on myself. I also like Aaron Copland's *Appalachian Spring* because it's so lively. It perks up your mood. After listening to it you can't be sad.

—Anonymous

One of my favorite singers is Johnny Mathis. I love his songs "Chances Are" and "The Twelfth of Never." His singing always gave me hope that there was love out there for me. I also believed I could love someone as well as the words said, if someone could just see.

—Jackie, 63, Bloomington, IL
(nurse/teacher)

I like classical music. I consider everything else just noise. Well, almost! My favorite pieces are Beethoven's "6th Symphony" and Mozart's "Opus 40." They soothe my soul. I also think Beethoven solved complex math in music with superb mastery and created works that will be listened to till the end of the world.

—**Arkan, 67, Newark, DE**
(engineer)

There's comfort in Big Band music with lots of trumpet, like Benny Goodman and the Dorsey brothers. This is real "lift yourself up" music, which reminds me of the house I used to visit as a child. The father was a trumpet player and we would hear him practice. The house seemed like a safe haven.

—**Nancy, 43, New York, NY**
(artist)

Listening to Pachelbel's "Canon in D" with my entire body. Taking in the divine harmony with every cell reminds me of the sacred mystery called music. I find that comforting.

—**C. Diane, 54, Tucson, AZ**
(writer/healer)

Saturday morning is opera day for me. To get ready to listen to other people stressing their lungs on the Metropolitan Opera stage 3,000 miles away, I awake early and head to the Santa Monica Mountains. There, far from everything civilized, I climb rosemary-scented hillsides, dazzled by the rising morning sunlight, until I reach hills above the clouds. In my cathedral, I look down upon the shoreline curling around the sea. I am breathing deeply, inhaling this view I share with no one. When I finally descend in time to arrive home, shower and turn on the radio, I know for me there is no better way to prepare my soul for the communion of a weekend.

—Dale, 63, Venice, CA
(filmmaker/writer)

The Beatles have the power to alter my mood, particularly in bad traffic. If I'm fuming and frustrated and helpless on the 405 Freeway, let a Beatles song—any Beatles song—come on the radio, and I am at once happier and calmer. I will go from angry or sad to happy, if only for two minutes and fifty-nine seconds. I usually turn up the volume, often joining in on vocals. I might roll down the window to share the wonder of the Beatles with my fellow drivers. Hear them? Hear how stupendous they are? How their music bursts with everything that is right with the world? Call it nostalgia, a feeble attempt to regain lost innocence or cling to the past, it doesn't really matter. Amidst the exhaust fumes, car horns, rude drivers and snail-paced lanes of traffic, the Beatles' music is salvation.

—Wendy, 50, Los Angeles, CA
(receptionist by day, writer/filmmaker by heart)

I need music—the "Easter Chorus" from *Cavalleria Rusticana* never fails to renew my spirits. Beethoven is always good. His "Pastoral Symphony" soothes and surrounds and uplifts. The act of singing itself can bring instant relief when I am low. I think it takes energy and focus. You get distracted hauling up notes and lyrics and voilà! When you finish, you have forgotten what made you so blue.

—Sheila, 62, Cincinnati, OH
(photographer)

I love any Helen Reddy CD because it reminds me I am a strong, independent, intelligent woman of power.

—Kerry, 28, Brooklyn, NY
(counselor)

Listening to jazz brings me comfort. Miles Davis' *Kind of Blue*—without fail for getting stress-busting, comfort-inducing attitude adjustment.

—Mike, 31, Hudson, MA
(advertising executive)

I like to play guitar. I like romantic music. I don't play very well…but I try.

—Valentin, 28, Spring Valley, NY
(horse groomer)

Claire de Lune by Debussy fills my soul with joy. There's an endless optimism that the music seems to be communicating. I picture nymphs dancing around cool pools of water. Then again, I also picture fat bald men dancing in the streets in great good cheer. Everyone is invited to celebrate the simplicity, the beauty of pure audio comfort. If you don't believe me, pop it in the CD player the next time you feel like terrorists have destroyed all that is good, pure and innocent in the world. You will find otherwise.

—**Robert, 28, Oberlin, OH**
(assistant artistic director)

My favorite CD is by the Benedictine monks of Santo Domingo de Silos. The chanting sounds so beautiful and has a calming effect on me.

—**Erika, 28 Bronx, NY**
(office superwoman)

My Comfort Music

_____

_____

_____

_____

_____

_____

_____

_____

_____

_____

Surround yourself with people

who respect and treat you well.

—Claudia Black
(psychotherapist/author)

People

The memory of my parents gives me the most comfort. Their untiring efforts on my behalf, the brave inconsistencies of effort they made to make life comfortable and meaningful for our family; the small things, the political/cultural differences they negotiated on our behalf; the deference they made to make adults out of children–with words we make these acts seem remarkable, but as acts they were invisible, sacrificial and virtuous. Godlike.

—Ed, 51, Norwood, MA
(English and film teacher)

I remember my grandmother a lot. It was she who taught me so much and was such a fine example of what love, tenderness and honesty meant.

—Anonymous

I talk with friends. I listen, especially to the elderly. One person, a neighbor, had a tremendous effect. He held the elevator doors open for me one day, looked into my eyes and said, "Don't retreat! Don't retreat!" I saw it as a call to take some action.

—Jane, Richmond, VA
(friend)

My children bring me joy and comfort. I look at them and I'm amazed that these two young men started as tiny embryos in my body. They've enriched my life and have taught me many valuable lessons.

—Nilda, 46, New York, NY
(legal advocate)

I have a friend who likes me even when I'm at my most stupid, even when I'm feeling fat, even when I want to stay inside and sulk. She knows when to let me be and when to coax me out into life. I'm grateful for her presence and persistence.

—Beth, 55, Miami, FL
(painter)

What comforts me is being with people I love, eating French fries and drinking Pisco sours (Chilean beverage with Pisco–a distilled grape drink).

—**Patricio, 32, Torres del Paine, Chile
(tour guide)**

I like to call my angels, people who bring out the best in me, people who listen but are not judgmental. These are the people I turn to when I'm down.

—**Anonymous**

When I need to feel young again, I go play with my kids, ages 6 and 8. They always remind me of what is really important in life and how to enjoy life to its fullest.

—**Bob, 46, Riverside, CA
(psychologist)**

My therapist has been a good mother, mentor, role model and an imperfectly real person. How wonderfully refreshing and lucky for me.

—**Trudy, 45, Chicago, IL
(real estate broker)**

When I'm most in need I make sure I surround myself with loving friends and family, who know how to laugh and be silly until my stomach hurts and tears come to my eyes.

—Susan, 55, New York, NY
(program director)

What comforts me is to be with people who know and accept who I am, understand my circumstances and needs and have in themselves a sense of compassion, understanding and caring. Companionship from family and friends does just that.

—Barry, 60, Acton, MA
(engineer)

I like being around strong women. Sharing experiences and ideas with them is important because then I know I'm not alone. Sometimes just being in the company of others, even if you're just sitting there not functioning, not talking or interacting, just not being alone, can be comforting.

—Courtney, Cottonwood, AZ
(cook)

The thought of Nelson Mandela is a comfort–almost forty years in a South African prison fighting a regime and political system that was dehumanizing and unjust. He had/has enough strength of character and compassion not to be bitter about his experience. He is a shining example of human greatness.

—Daniel, 32, Providence, RI
(entrepreneur)

My family–partner, son and daughter–comforts me because they cuddle, hug and feel good. We have a comfortable knowing of each other and a history as well as a future together. They are a constant affirmation of the delight, security, challenge and necessity of an open heart.

—Kathryn, Newark, DE

I try to remember a person who was good to me and allow the sounds, smells, feelings and sights to surround the image and be in that lovely moment with that person in my thoughts.

—Sally, 64, Danbury, CT
(teacher/actress)

I get home from work about an hour after my wife. I walk into the kitchen, she's reading at the table or standing by the stove. She walks over to me, stands on tiptoe and kisses me on the forehead, cheeks, nose and lips. I love the sameness of this everyday greeting, the warmth and familiarity of her touch.

—Walter, 42, Burlington, VT
(high school teacher/poet)

A good talk with an old friend concerning the vicissitudes of life, good and/or bad times. The connection and the continuity of our relationship keep feelings of loneliness and isolation at bay.

—Barbara, Hartford, CT
(person on earth)

Being in the presence of my mother is comforting. She doesn't have to be in the room or in the house. It is her essence. Nothing can touch me. I'm fully accepted. I'm a bare-naked baby.

—Dwarym, 28, Staten Island, NY
(human being)

I call my childhood friend on the West Coast. She is incredibly sensitive and supportive and loving. I only see her once a year and we talk maybe eight times a year but we're still very close. Somehow, connecting with someone who's known me all my life makes me feel very good.

—Margo, 39, New York, NY
(TV production)

Being with good friends. This has always been the number one comforter and it seems to be more so since 9/11. Knowing that people I care for were safe that day and since then has become even more important. It gives me a sense of security that is comforting.

—Janet, 65, New York, NY
(retired psychologist)

My Comfort People

Name   Telephone Number

_____

_____

_____

_____

_____

_____

_____

_____

Name	Telephone Number

Action is the antidote to despair.

– Joan Baez
(singer/songwriter)

Actions

When I do something physical like hike, run, dance or exercise, I feel I gain ownership of my body. This feeling grounds me.

—Jennifer, 40, New York, NY
(professional musician/law student)

I exercise. It's grueling at first but I feel so much better once it's over. I always feel I accomplished something good for myself.

—Melanie, 25, New York, NY
(teacher)

I clean. Not just straightening up, but hard-core organizing. Getting rid of things I don't need makes me feel great. If I haven't used or worn it in a year, it's out.

—Zoe, 24, Montclair, NJ
(aerobics teacher)

Whenever I can, I take a yoga class. It's so relaxing. It helps stop the noise in my head and makes me feel good about my body. It's healing as well as an "exercise." It helps me focus and concentrate.

—Lynn, 43, New York, NY
(occupational therapy assistant)

I read the Bible and pray to God. I talk to God like I would a friend. My faith keeps me strong, especially when I go through tough times.

—Jazmin, 27, Bronx, NY
(legal advocate)

Buying and arranging flowers tells me that I can create something beautiful and then have it to look at.

—Bonnie, 61, New York, NY
(retired psychotherapist)

Knitting connects me to my mother (long since gone) and this connection brings me solace. I also find comfort in silence because it centers me.

—Mary, 62, Norwalk, CT
(retired nurse)

There is comfort in knowing I can pay my bills.

—Sarah, 38, New York, NY
(mother)

Meditation and prayer have always been endless sources
of comfort for me, whether it's sitting alone in the quiet
of my room, listening to chants or being in a sanctuary.
Reading the Gospel of John, verse 14, always works.

—Susan, 55, New York, NY
(program director)

When I feel overwhelmed I ask myself, "Is there anything I can do about it right this minute?" Many times
the answer is "No" and that helps me to relax and keep
my perspective.

—Sharon, 55, Lawrence, MA
(children's activities director)

Deep breathing helps me connect with my body when
my thoughts become confused.

—Anonymous

Holding myself is comforting. I'll wrap my arms around myself and lay down on my couch or bed. It's a reminder I give myself that I am loved.

—Tina, 20, Hoboken, NJ
(secretary)

I stare and meditate on a candle. I look at the flame and imagine that heat inside of me, warming me, soothing me, calming.

—Amy, Brooklyn, NY

Going to the beauty parlor comforts me. I'll get my hair and nails done. These things make me feel good about myself and that feeling, that I look well no matter what's going on, that I'm put together, brings me comfort.

—Shirley, 24, New York, NY
(project assistant)

Trading back rubs with a friend—but not on the same day!

—Carol, 41, Pittsburgh, PA
(lawyer)

I sing a favorite song loud and with as much energy as I can offer. This helps to release/relieve negative energy or any anger I may be feeling.

—Elizabeth, 40, New York, NY
(case manager)

Working hard and making good money comforts me, along with knowing that I live in the greatest country in the world.

—Mark, 45, New York, NY
(accountant)

I make a collage out of…anything. The cutting, ripping and gluing can be very satisfying.

—Marina, 40, Natick, MA
(partner, crafts gallery)

Doing volunteer work is satisfying when my self-esteem is low because it gives me a chance to help others and feel valuable and useful in the process.

—Joyce, 39, San Francisco, CA
(saleswoman)

Sometimes when I'm stressed I find comfort in ordinary tasks like washing dishes or going to the Laundromat. These are simple things, and when I've finished them I can be satisfied with the job I've done and feel that at least this aspect of my life is in order.

—John, 35, Stamford, CT
(stockbroker)

Throwing I Ching coins comforts me by giving me a ritual that feels powerful and connected to Spirit. The result or reading is almost always something that helps me find insight or hope. I also take long drives in my Mustang. I crank up the music—usually rock and roll—and drive with no destination in mind. I do some of my best thinking and praying in the car.

—Jan, 51, Cottonwood, AZ
(counselor)

I walk to the Hudson River, take a notebook with me and do one of two things. I write a letter listing things/ideas/people/experiences I want to say goodbye to, or a letter of wishes/prayers (things I'd like to happen in my life or for other people). I then take the letter, fold it up, attach it to a rock or heavy object and toss it into the water. I watch it get swept away until I can't see it any longer. It's a great thing to do anytime or especially on New Year's Day or any other day of beginnings and endings.

—Cara, 29, New York, NY
(actress)

I visualize God's hands, cupped and open in a receiving manner. I place my problems there—cut all strings attached—watch God's hands close, and say a prayer of thanks.

—Anonymous

I run a hot bath and pour as much bubble bath as the tub can stand without overflowing, and I soak while looking at catalogues that I'd never shop from for one reason or another.

—Karen, 34, Westfield, NJ
(social worker)

Talking online with school friends makes me feel
not lonely.

—Christopher, 13, Bronx, NY
(student)

It comforts me to fantasize what I'd do if I won the Lotto
(send my entire family to psychotherapy, travel the
world, build the perfect house).

—Danette, 46, Kew Gardens, NY
(restaurant owner/social worker)

Comfort is going IN—through meditation, journey work
or soul hunting—getting to that place where you cease to
exist, yet exist in the fullest way in oneness with the
divine/the universe. There are a number of routes you
can take, but they all lead to that same place, and when
you're there you feel comfortable in your own skin. If
you are not aware of your body, you feel comfortable
with your soul. For me, this is really the ultimate comfort.

—Sally, 44, New York, NY
(trance-dance facilitator)

The one thing I can say is that if I'm in a traumatic or uncomfortable situation with no comforting things around me...I find comfort in knowing that it's not going to last and everything eventually will be okay.

**—Kerry, 24, North Arlington, NJ
(inside sales/office manager)**

I like to take long naps on weekends. All troubles are forgotten when I finally give in to the tiredness in my body and the sleep in my eyes. I wake up emotionally restored and clear-headed. Even if you don't sleep, just being cozy in bed in the middle of the day feels rejuvenating and safe.

**—Ruth, 54, Bronx, NY
(psychotherapist)**

"Puttering" is good; doing small jobs like cleaning up an old fishing reel, repairing a broken lamp, fixing a leaky faucet. These activities are comforting because they're engaging, they hold my attention and they are doable. They're not demanding and yet they each offer at least a modicum of self-satisfaction and a feeling of accomplishment.

**—Howard, 62, Stephenstown, NY
(psychoanalyst)**

I write really, really angry letters to people I don't like,
then rip them up and flush them down the toilet.

—Jack, 15, St. Louis, MO
(student)

Swimming laps. For thirty to sixty minutes you move
every muscle, you get loose, you cannot answer the
phone or otherwise be interrupted, your mind can go
here and there (especially when you use the clock rather
than count laps). You feel great immediately afterward
and you sleep more deeply that night. It's opposite in
many ways from my tension-producing activities: sitting
at a computer writing or editing on a deadline.

—Rick, 57, Los Angeles, CA
(creator of marketing materials)

I was never one of those people who liked the Christmas
family newsletter. But since 9/11 I decided I wanted to be
more in touch, more involved with my family and
friends. I began to send a monthly report (I write and
send it the last week of the month) to seven relatives and
five friends. I write about what's going on with my family,

anything new or interesting I've seen, read or done. It's about sharing more of myself with others. It makes me feel better.

—Mark, 36, Greenwich, CT
(lawyer)

I love having my head stroked—I think because it's probably a very early baby thing and, as an incest survivor, makes it clear to me that my head, not (just) my body, is valued.

—Julia, 56, New York, NY
(lawyer)

I'm very good at shopping for others. It's gratifying to come up with something "thoughtful"—useful but economical. It gives me tremendous pleasure if I can figure out somebody else's desire…although they might never have actually formulated it.

—George, 50, Piedmont, CA
(consultant)

I read the newspaper every day from cover to cover. It occupies my mind. It puts me at ease to know what's happening in the world. I feel more relaxed knowing what's going on in my immediate city surroundings.

—Maurice, 58, New York, NY
(salesman)

For physical comfort, i.e. when I am ill, I like solitude and silence. I believe I can focus my energies onto my illness when I concentrate on trying to heal it, so being alone and undistracted is a help.

—Daniela

Working out brings me comfort. Doing yoga, running or lifting weights, depending on what I'm in the mood for. Each of these activities allows me to go inside my body to deal with whatever feelings I may be having that are difficult. At the end of a workout it sometimes feels like I'm wringing myself out like a sponge soaked in stress, pain, anger, etc. I just let it all go.

—Andrew, 28, Brooklyn, NY
(graduate student)

I will do any physical activity that takes my mind away from whatever troubles me. I'll play tennis, shoot hoops and go Rollerblading.

—Carlos, 56, New York, NY
(schoolteacher)

Long, hot showers are comforting. It feels like I'm washing away the literal and figurative accumulated dirt of the day.

—Jill, 36, New York, NY
(graduate student)

Sex is comforting because sexual intimacy helps me feel connected and close—not alone.

—Abby, 51, New York, NY
(social worker)

I love to treat people to things. Whether it's a baseball game for all my college roommates, a round of drinks for friends, dinner for the whole family or a special surprise gift for my wife. It just plain makes me feel like a million bucks and brings me great joy to say, "I got it!"

—Kevin, 33, Waltham, MA
(advertising executive)

Talking on the phone to my girlfriend in California comforts me. I miss her and she calms me down. She gives me good advice and I know that someone is on my side.

—Danny, 22, Bronx, NY
(comedian)

Holding babies. I love babies, even when they're crying. Love the feel, smell, look of them. The feeling when they nuzzle in the crook of my neck. I find them so interesting–I could watch and interact with them for hours. For the last two years I've done weekly volunteering cuddling sick babies at a local hospital. It brings me comfort to comfort others.

—Cheryl, 50, New York, NY

Checking any item off "The List"–whether a huge project at work, re-carpeting the basement, finishing a photo album or writing a letter. The act of accomplishing a task I wanted to accomplish brings me great comfort.

—Nicolas, 36, Waltham, MA
(president of own firm)

The computer is something I have control over. The challenge is getting it to work right. I like figuring out what's wrong and finding a remedy. It gives me a sense of satisfaction.

—Ralph, 50, Bronx, NY
(dad)

In the last year I've discovered an area of ability and skill that was heretofore unknown to me. It emerged with fixing up an old house my wife and I bought. I find great comfort and accomplishment in working on the house, be it painting, hanging fixtures, stripping and refinishing furniture, plastering walls, etc. It all feels terribly creative and nice when I've taken something old or in disrepair and made it look like new...or just good.

—Shelly, 53, New York, NY
(psychologist)

My Comfort Actions

_____

_____

_____

_____

_____

_____

_____

_____

_____

_____

All animals except man

know that the ultimate of life

is to enjoy it.

—Samuel Butler
(author)

Animals

Animals! A relationship with an animal is what comes immediately to my mind when seeking solace. Dogs, particularly, offer comfort and warmth without ever asking a stupid question or uttering an insensitive comment. I can think of nothing more heartening than the animal world at those terrible times when the human world is at its most brutish.

—Elizabeth, 47, New York, NY
(playwright)

Stroking and combing my cats, soothing them, is soothing to me.

—Bonnie, 61, New York, NY
(retired psychotherapist)

Pets seem to have a sixth sense that tells them when you need them the most, and they respond to it. They love you unconditionally, regardless of what happens to you.

—Anne, 43, North Andover, MA
(secretary)

My pet always comforts me. I can talk and cry and complain and just exhaust myself from pent-up emotions, and my pet will just sit there and kiss me.

—Sandy, Pleasantville, NY

Being in the presence of my pet, doing things with her, just out walking in the park, seeing her happy is a terrifically gratifying experience. It always makes me feel better.

—Naomi, 48, New York, NY
(psychoanalyst)

My cat Moby is my comfort. Even if I've had the worst day—full of stress and conflict—he's unconditionally psyched to see me when I walk through the door.

—Tod, 40, Westfield, NJ
(attorney)

Recently I had the privilege of riding a mule. This animal wore my person on his body. There was a time when we rested by the side of the road and I fed him carrots. When I looked into his eyes I felt acceptance. I felt he said to me, "If you are going to ride on my back, then you need to realize and accept the aches and pains that may be a result of that." A life lesson.

—Charlotte, Cottonwood, AZ

Comfort is having a purring cat lie on my stomach, arm or feet. The warmth and calmness of the cat makes me feel loved and secure.

—Barbara, 56, Brooklyn, NY

I enjoy sparring with my Jack Russell terrier. He knows it's a game and attacks my hands with energy and enthusiasm. It's amazing that he never goes too far and will stop when I switch to a gentle touch. Smart dog.

—Bob, 51, Pompton Plains, NJ
(horseshoer)

Birds outside my window. I have a bird feeder and love to see sparrows and gray doves feasting. I so enjoy their songs. This gives me comfort. Most of all, my heart skips a beat when a hummingbird feeds off one of my hanging plants. Oh, the comfort of God's many gifts.

**—Marie, 58, Santa Monica, CA
(actress/writer/producer/editor/teacher/work-in-progress)**

Spring can bring quite a bit of joy for everybody, but for me, the joy is focused on one thing: baby animals. Goslings, to be exact. In the spring of 2000, I became ill and had to take a three-month leave of absence from my work. As I recovered, I would visit the park every day to watch the babies' progress. In many ways, I felt like we were growing together as I found my footing again. Now every year, I look forward to seeing my fuzzy yellow friends hatching and pecking at everything in sight. It brings me a lot of comfort to know it's never too late to be reborn.

**—Aminda, 25, Ridgefield Park, NJ
(graduate student)**

I like hanging out with all of my pets (five cats, two dogs). Animals are very cathartic as they reach a level inside me that is very bare, real and true. They offer unconditional love and a basic sense of trust that I don't believe is completely inherent within humans. They offer comfort and solace and incite a need in me to become a better person.

—Lysa, 39, Los Angeles, CA
(nurse)

Cat holding is an important comforting activity for me—daily. I love the softness of their fur, the soothing purr, the "I trust you and you're a good kitty mom" sense of having my cat rest her head against my shoulder. Time and the world stop, and holding is all that matters to either of us.

—C. Diane, 54, Tucson, AZ
(writer/healer)

My Comfort Animals

_____

_____

_____

_____

_____

_____

_____

_____

_____

_____

I go to nature to be soothed and healed

and to have my senses put in order.

— John Burroughs
(naturalist, writer)

Nature

I love sitting on a bench by the water, watching the sun go down and seeing the sky and water become one.

—Erika, 28, Bronx, NY
(office superwoman)

I go outdoors, watch the sky and breathe in gulpfuls of air. The planet goes on no matter what happens to us. It is eternal.

—Jennifer, 40, New York, NY
(professional musician/law student)

I let myself contemplate a star and try to reach it in thought. I allow the vastness of the universe to fill me with awe.

—Sally, 64, Danbury, CT
(teacher/actress)

I watch the sun rise each morning, bringing a fresh start, and I have hope that some things will change this day.

—Barbara, 63, Norwalk, CT
(retired social worker)

Being outside helps me connect with my spirit. Hiking in the forest engages the little kid in me who loves to explore.

—Joyce, 39, San Francisco, CA
(saleswoman)

Just stopping, standing still to look up at the sky, especially when I'm rushing around the city, calms me.

—Christine, 49, New York, NY
(social worker)

Basically any landscape that dwarfs me comforts me.

—Cathy, 39, Salisbury, CT
(photographer)

Central Park. New York City. Spring. When I see the forsythia and daffodils in bloom, I am hopeful.

—Donna, 37, New York, NY
(singer)

Swishing through a heavy leaf fall, kicking swirls of leaves into the air engenders the sense that I am a part of my earthly environment.

—Barbara, Hartford, CT
(person on earth)

The sun, sometimes. Warmth always comforts me. For some reason, I associate fear and pain with being physically cold, and when I'm lying in the sun, in the park or on the beach, I feel very relaxed. Sometimes—it is hard to describe well because the moments are so vague and ephemeral and rare—there's a quality to the light, or a fragrance in the air, and I will be brought to tears and just be so completely overcome by the absolute beauty of the world and the joy of being alive in it. And, for that moment, just being aware of and being able to experience that beauty more than makes up for any of the pain or sorrow or suffering that might have come before or will come in the future. It's as though just for a second, the world makes sense.

—Samantha, 26, New York, NY
(film publicist)

To lift my spirits...besides a big smile from a pretty girl...or a big hug from Mom, Dad or Sis... a great sunset, sunrise or watching the stars makes me feel real.

—Matt, 33, Boulder, CO
(sales rep)

Storms. The sound of rain falling is soothing. It calms my soul. Rain symbolizes a new beginning. It's most comforting when you're sheltered, but you can see and hear its immense power.

—Aris, 22, Toronto, Canada
(student)

I love summer rain when you're caught off guard and soaked but you just don't care. This is an amazing experience for me because you can't change it but you can enjoy it.

—Denise, 36, Brookline, MA
(real estate broker)

The good comfort is the kind that calms one down in a healthy, perhaps even quasi-spiritual kinda way...walking in the woods and just thinking...listening to the sounds of

the winds, and birds and bugs…looking intensely at everything…the coloration and texture on the bark of a
tree…the intricate veins in a leaf…the way the sunlight
hits certain branches.

—Darby, 45, Bronx, NY
(drama therapist)

When my mind is racing and I'm feeling anxious…the
best thing for me to do is go for a hike. Everything
seems to slow down. I feel I'm sane again. Not only the
physical aspect of the hike, but nature itself, the wind
and the sun, seems to have a calming effect on me.

—George, 50, Piedmont, CA
(consultant)

Being in nature provides great relief and peace of mind
for me. I am next to the youngest of ten children. If you
wanted to be alone you had to go outside. My favorite
spot was up in a tree that overlooked the whole neighborhood. I can't climb trees like when I was young, but I
find great comfort in sitting under them.

—Jan, 51, Cottonwood, AZ
(counselor)

My Comfort in Nature

_____

_____

_____

_____

_____

_____

_____

_____

_____

_____

Asking for Comfort

Sometimes, in order to get the comfort you need, you have to go outside of yourself and invite other people in. Take a few minutes to figure out what you really need and/or want specifically, and then make an "I" statement to the individual who can fulfill your request.

I.   Identify your comfort need.

II.   Choose an appropriate person to ask for help.

III.   Make an "I" statement (some samples are "I need...," "I want...," "I would like you to...")

IV.   See what happens.

V.   The success is in the asking.

Practice your "I" statements here: e.g. "I'm tired. I'd like you to be the one to make weekend plans."

_____

_____

_____

_____

_____

_____

_____

_____

_____

_____

Comfort Worksheets

How to find your comfort

I

Think about what brought you comfort as a child.
(Write down your thoughts.)

Ask family and friends what they do to lift their spirits.
(Think about their answers.)

Try on different ideas and suggestions and see what fits
and feels good.

Continue to ask yourself, "What is it that makes me feel
better physically, emotionally, spiritually?"

Make a list of comfort ideas and tape that list to your
refrigerator or bathroom mirror.

Be conscious of your comfort ideas before you need them.

How to find your comfort

II

Sit in a quiet place.

Ask yourself, "What brings me comfort?"

Breathe in.

Exhale slowly through your mouth.

Listen for your answers.

Repeat.

Comfort Smells

Freshly ground coffee. Chocolate chip cookies right out of the oven. Bay Rum pipe tobacco. Shalimar. Freshly mowed grass. Smells that just smell good...because they do. And smells that evoke fond memories of time and place.

What smells bring you comfort?

_____

_____

_____

_____

_____

_____

_____

General Comfort

This page is for you to list your comforts in general (i.e. fireplaces, hugs, sunsets, mashed potatoes, hot chocolate with marshmallows, herbal tea, cheesecake, scented candles, potpourri, cashmere anything, massages).

_____

_____

_____

_____

_____

_____

_____

Questionnaire

Dear Reader:

You can help add to the Comfort Project by sharing specific things that bring you comfort (i.e. favorite book, movie, quote, song, place, food, etc.) and *why* they're important to you. Include as many ideas as you like. (Please copy this page and send to Jane Seskin, c/o Tallfellow Press, 1180 S. Beverly Drive, Los Angeles, CA 90035.) Thank you.

1. _____

_____

_____

_____

2. _____

_____

_____

_____

3. _____

_____

_____

_____

4. _____

_____

_____

_____

5. _____

_____

_____

Personal Information (optional)

Name _____

Age _____

City/State_____

Occupation _____

Jane Seskin is a psychotherapist, social worker and writer living in New York City. For the past 16 years she has worked at the Crime Victims Treatment Center of St. Luke's Roosevelt Hospital, specializing in domestic violence. She is a frequent speaker, supervisor and consultant to police departments, community boards, hospitals and social service agencies. She also conducts a private practice, dealing with family relationships, depression, alcoholism, divorce and bereavement.